SEA POWER

SEA POWER

ADMIRAL OF THE FLEET THE
LORD HILL-NORTON
and John Dekker

faber and faber

First published in 1982
by Faber and Faber Limited
3 Queen Square London WC1N 3AU
Filmset by Latimer Trend & Company Ltd, Plymouth
Printed in Great Britain by
Fakenham Press Ltd, Fakenham, Norfolk

British Library Cataloguing in Publication Data

Hill-Norton, Peter, Baron Hill-Norton
  Sea power.
  1. Great Britain. Royal Navy—History
  I. Title II. Dekker, John
  359′.00941 VA454

ISBN 0–571–11890–9

CONTENTS

? Corvettes ?

PLATES

ACKNOWLEDGEMENTS

Of the many distinguished scholars in whose debt we must always be, two names especially stand out: those of Captain Stephen Roskill, Royal Navy, all of whose works, and especially his truly great history of the war at sea, are filled with wise observations and reflections, as might be expected of one who fought his ship with gallantry in that same conflict; and of Arthur J. Marder, best remembered perhaps for his monumental work *From the Dreadnought to Scapa Flow* and for *The Anatomy of British Sea Power*. We also owe a debt of gratitude to Paul Kennedy of the University of East Anglia, who was historical adviser to the television series on which this book is based and, indeed, suggested the structure we have adopted.

Our grateful thanks are due to the staff of the Naval Historical Branch for their skill and patience in answering our inquiries. Gwenyth Thomas typed the manuscript, prepared the index and dealt with both of us with infinite patience and skill.

We alone, of course, must be held accountable for the accuracy of the facts and for the opinions expressed in these pages.

PREFACE

The origin of this book is to be found in a series of television documentary films that we made together about sea power. We have written the book on the same lines (though that is by no means the only way of doing it) because sea power is essentially about navies, which comprise different types of warship. We could have arranged our book by weapons systems, or we could have attempted a straightforward historical approach; but the ordering of the story according to warship type is, we think, a logical one, and besides, we have not tried to write definitive history. Nor is this a book for the warship 'buff', since the warship type is of interest to us only for the purpose it has served; what follows, therefore, is neither textbook nor history book. It is about sea power and its principal instruments.

Our book necessarily contains some of the history, on the following lines. The chapter entitled 'Battleship' includes a description of what went before the *Dreadnought* as well as what came after; and we have tried to explain why, for a very long time, the concept of the battle-fleet was central to the thinking of *all* naval planners. This part of the story overlaps with others because the battle-fleet always put to sea with other types of warship in attendance, but we have, as far as possible, confined ourselves to the principal type within each chapter. For example, that glamorous maverick of naval warfare, the battle-cruiser, has been put where she properly belongs, in the cruiser family.

'Carrier', the third chapter, might have been called 'Maritime Aviation, Ship-Borne and Shore-Based', but we trust the shorter title will serve as long as one thinks of maritime airfields ashore as stationary and unsinkable aircraft-carriers, so we make no apology for treating maritime air power as part of sea power. The 'Gunboat' story is about the sloop-type, yesterday's monitor and armed landing craft, the river gunboat and coast-defence ship of the day before yesterday and the fishery protection vessel of today. Thus the shore-bombardment function and the maritime policing task are treated in the same chapter for reasons of history.

Chapter Five, 'Commando', is about a concept, not a warship type, because to call this chapter 'Landing Craft' or 'Assault Ship' would have been both pedantic and too restrictive. We have attempted to describe the idea of amphibious warfare in the context of sea power, which is that of holding troops over the horizon, then bringing them swiftly to the battlefield endowed with sufficient fire-power and tactical mobility, something that only a 'blue-water' navy can do. Although the idea fell into disuse at the beginning of this century and came into fashion again only very recently, it is now a concept well understood by the navies of the super-powers and the medium powers too.

The cruiser (discussed in Chapter Six) may have surrendered many of her duties to aircraft and satellites, but she remains recognizable as a type, even though today's destroyers and frigates rival her in size and function. There is nothing new in this, however, since changes in title were common enough a century and a half ago.

Chapter Seven, 'Submarine', is three stories in one, being an account of the diesel electric submersible that was so effective in two wars and of the two types of true submarine, the strategic nuclear ballistic-missile platform and the very large attack ('hunter-killer') boat, both nuclear-powered.

In 'Destroyer' we describe the evolution of the torpedo-boat destroyer into outsize torpedo-boat and miniature cruiser, the almost parallel development of the anti-submarine vessel and, eventually, the general-purpose destroyer and frigate. It is the most difficult warship to write about because destroyers have been employed for every conceivable naval purpose. We could have written a separate chapter about the torpedo-boat, and her descendants, the motor-torpedo-boat and the fast patrol boat, but we have been strongly influenced by the British experience—one of us has served in the Royal Navy for half a century—and in the past hundred years that navy has more often than not found itself on the defensive against such craft. The argument thus leads back to 'Destroyer'. The mine-sweeper and her much more expensive granddaughter, the mine counter-measures vessel, deserve more than passing mention here because we have deliberately said little about them in the text. For a very long time the mine has been a cheap means of defence, very much the weapon of the weaker naval power. As an offensive weapon it is now more dangerous than ever to a maritime nation, though the method of defence has always been primarily to frustrate the offensive mine-layer, and that has usually been the task of the destroyer.

One more point: this book is about warship types and their employment in the struggle for sea power. It does not include a description of the machinery of command in the Royal Navy or in any other navy, which deserves a book to itself, as does the elaborate and comprehensive supply organization for the navy which owes so much to Samuel Pepys. Some aspects of the command structure of the Royal Navy will become apparent in these pages, if only because the Admiralty was always an operational headquarters as well as an administrative one, unlike the War Office and Air Ministry, until the quite recent reorganization of that part of the machinery of government which deals with defence.

P. J. H.-N.
J. D.

Chapter One

SIZE AND SHAPE

The Navy, whereon, under the good Providence of God, the wealth, safety and strength of the Kingdom chiefly depend....

Articles of War, 1661

Geography compels some nations to be concerned with sea power. Britain is a truly maritime nation, the British an island people whose very life depends on foreign trade which is almost entirely sea-borne. A vast natural breakwater some 600 miles in length, a huge 'unsinkable aircraft-carrier', Britain stands athwart the approaches to Western Europe, and for centuries this island barrier and British sea power have combined to frustrate the attempts of Continental powers to reach out across the oceans. Those same powers have in turn attempted, and sometimes all but succeeded, in disrupting Britain's maritime commerce and so threatening the very safety and wealth of the realm. It is not surprising that Britain has had a navy for so long.

Properly employed, British sea power has supported and sustained British, and often Allied, military power, as in the Seven Years' War, in the Napoleonic Wars and in the two great wars of the twentieth century. Today the defence of Britain is also the defence of Europe. It is a defence in depth, which extends far into the broad Atlantic Ocean, where the great convoy battles were fought, and across the narrow seas, where for centuries the struggle has been no less fierce in battles against the Spanish, French, Dutch and German navies. To defend Europe by land or by sea alone is impossible. The two modes are complementary, and armies and navies must share a common strategy. Today Britain's navy is still the world's third largest— after those of the two super-powers. It is also the only other major 'blue-water' navy, able to fight far out in the oceans to provide that defence in depth. The most powerful navy in Europe, and the most experienced, its contribution to European security is unique and irreplaceable.

The idea of sea power has seldom been taken very seriously, even in a maritime nation such as Britain. It is true that most people vaguely believe in British sea power rather as they do in Christianity; the Royal Navy is rather like the Anglican Church—comfortable to have in the background but receiving close attention only in times of trouble. The Royal Navy has always stood high in the public regard, while few people ever bother to ask what the Navy is *for*, what it is expected to *do*, and, more important, what it *can* do. This state of affairs is not new; in the 1880s there was the same general lack of understanding about sea power. Much the same unquestioning complacency was to be found in the Royal Navy itself. Few officers then had much idea of what they were expected to do, except to 'show the flag' around the world, and indeed, in the century between the Battle of Trafalgar and the Battle of Tsushima 'showing the flag' was an important duty for the Royal Navy, a duty for which it was reasonably well equipped. The pace of technical innovation and the shock of twentieth-century warfare have changed all that. Twice in one generation Britain's maritime links with the rest of the world have almost been severed. Twice her people have endured isolation and have even faced the prospect of starvation and defeat at the hands of a Continental enemy just across the narrow seas. On both occasions Britain had a large navy with a wealth of fighting experience and an abundance of professional skill and confidence, but on each occasion that navy was found unprepared for the threat which actually developed. Britain had the 'wrong-shaped' navy, designed and trained for the 'wrong kind' of war. Thus even after the Battle of Jutland, when the German battle-fleet was effectively shut up in harbour, Britain was almost defeated at sea by submarine warfare, and the story was to be repeated a quarter of a century later.

With hindsight, it is easy to apportion blame, but it is a comforting thought that other people also make mistakes. It now seems providential that both the Kaiser and Hitler encouraged the construction of a 'conventional' fleet of heavy surface ships, thus offering the Royal Navy and the British armaments industry a challenge they were well suited to meet; yet had Germany built an exclusively U-boat navy before either war,

Britain would still have been obliged to keep her own battleships and cruisers, since other naval powers possessed large surface fleets. While it now seems obvious that in 1939 the Royal Navy ought to have had fewer heavy warships, many more escort vessels and the long-range aircraft it has never been given, the Admiralty was aware of a range of threats of different kinds from at least three potential enemies. It is reasonable to suppose that since misjudgement (and even folly) were not the prerogatives of our ancestors alone, it is at least possible that similar misconceptions of danger may exist in present-day navies and Governments. A later generation will doubtless be better placed to explain the muddled thinking that has led to some of the errors committed by today's admirals and politicians in London, Washington or Moscow. There is, for example, no apparent reason why Admiral Gorshkov should have persuaded his masters of the need for very large cruisers. Are they seriously intended to fight the American carrier battle groups, or are they merely destined to be the world's most impressive gunboats ever? In his time Stalin spurred on the building of heavy cruisers, for which his immediate successors showed less enthusiasm, and it may well be that much of the present Soviet fleet is, for them, also the 'wrong-shaped' navy. What is of interest is that the Soviet navy has shown an understanding of some of the concepts of maritime warfare described in this book, though whether those concepts are relevant to its real needs only time will tell. To understand the growth of the American and Soviet navies and the contemporary decline of the British navy, it is helpful to place the story in its proper setting. Since any navy is composed of warships, with their aircraft and weapons systems, it is the size and shape of its warships that will indicate what that navy can be expected to do. Possession of a particular type of warship does not guarantee that the type will be employed in the manner expected: indeed, much of this book is about how navies have often employed their various types of warship quite wrongly, either through a misunderstanding of their strategic aims or because they had inherited a fleet designed for a different set of tasks. Thus it will be easier to see why some navies have developed the 'wrong shape' and how hard it is to determine what is the 'right shape'—and size—for a navy.

Of all the principal warship types described in this book, only one, the battleship, has for practical purposes disappeared, and certainly the concept of the battle-fleet action has gone for good.

All the rest remain in recognizable form, which is the more surprising considering the time span we have chosen, that of the past hundred years or so.

Such an arbitrary period is justifiable on several counts. The 1880s saw the beginning of the 'modern' naval era, not only in the appearance of the ships, already quite unrecognizable to the sailor of Nelson's time, but also in the breaking of the British monopoly of sea power, which for the preceding half-century had scarcely been challenged, even by France. From the 1880s, however, several European countries, the United States of America and, later, Japan were attaining industrial maturity. Some, like Germany, had recently become nation states, and all were about to transform their essentially coast-defence navies into powerful ocean-going fleets. Industrial capacity, newly acquired, facilitated the new sort of foreign policy that needed naval power to project national influence abroad, and, fortuitously, the pace of technical innovation created the means. Three-quarters of a century after Trafalgar the sailing ship had ceased to count as a man-of-war, and the steam engine had come fully of age. The beginnings of modern fire-power were manifest in long-range heavy guns, firing high-explosive, armour-piercing shells. Toughened steel armour-plate, all-steel hulls, subdivided into watertight compartments, were now accepted features of naval architecture. The armoured gun turret with a wide arc of fire had arrived.

By 1900 the armoured steel battle-fleet was unquestionably the chief instrument of sea power. Attended by cruisers, torpedo-boats, destroyers and, soon, the new submarines, the battle-fleet was, in every navy of importance, the main body destined to fight the decisive battle for command of the seas. The authority of the battle-fleet enabled the cruisers and the gunboats to police the oceans. Such was the doctrine that underpinned the creation of the British, German, American and other fleets at the turn of the century, and such was the philosophy that was to prevail for so long and is retained today by the strategic missile submarines and the carrier battle groups. The modern navy that began to appear a hundred years ago had several features that distinguished it from its forebears. Warships took less time to build, but they did not last as long, and anyway they fast became obsolete. But they could be bigger because naval architects were no longer limited by the size of a tree trunk and because steel was stronger than timber and almost as cheap. Yet the modern warship was vulnerable in ways the old line-of-battle ship was not, chiefly because of the destructive power of modern weapons. From the 1880s battleships—as they were now called—were expensive assets that could not be lightly risked. Fleet commanders developed a cautious outlook that would have seemed utterly foreign to admirals like Rodney and Nelson, although the old offensive spirit still motivated every officer in the fleet of 1914.

Advances in the technology of warship construction were accompanied by a series of arguments about the size and shape of warships that are familiar today. A discussion of sea power by reference to warship types invites two questions: why did the battleship, or the cruiser, or the destroyer acquire a particular size and shape? And why have some warship types almost disappeared? Our exercise in naval zoology is not undertaken because of a fascination with the past—though it is hard not to be in turn awed and intrigued by the truly colossal amount of energy, imagination and wealth that have been invested in warship construction during the past hundred years in Europe, America and Japan—it is undertaken, rather, because these questions are still being asked. The argument in the United States today is over whether Congress should fund the building of a very few large aircraft-carriers or several smaller ones. In the 1880s a very similar debate concerned the battleship, which was already thought by some to be out of date. Today British naval planners argue the merits of the smaller, cheaper anti-submarine frigate as against those of the larger, better armed but much more expensive version. Others, with no respectable evidence to support the view, contend that the ocean-going surface warship is out of date, having been superseded by the aircraft and the submarine—an argument first heard even before 1914!

The present debate about the size and shape of the Royal Navy in particular—although it is not the only navy under examination—is thus not new. Sometimes the language used has been intemperate. Compare the words of Admiral Sir Percy Scott, the true if not the 'onlie begetter' of modern naval gunnery, writing to *The Times* of 7 April 1922:

Naval men do not commit suicide, and battleships are vital to their profession and to their comfort. To be captain of a battleship is the ambition of every naval officer. Who else in the world travels about in the same comfort as the captain of a battleship?

and those of the *New Statesman* of 22 May 1981:

> The Royal Navy costs us about £2.5 billion a year, and what we get for the price is nothing like worthwhile. Two world wars (if nothing else) ought to have shown us that admirals, left unchecked, will always demonstrate an obsession with over-complicated, over-expensive and monumental items of naval architecture—together with practical contempt for the cheap and unglamorous vessels which are actually needed in a military crisis. Today's RN consists of a costly and highly vulnerable surface battle fleet, designed (if that's the word) to perish nobly in a North Atlantic *Götterdämmerung* which, practically speaking, couldn't take place until after the incineration of the majority of the British population. This has been supported at the cost of having: comically unsuitable ships for fishery and inshore protection; a mine counter-measures force which couldn't hope to keep our harbours clear from a Soviet mining operation (something which the USSR might just be able to threaten, one day, without having to cross the nuclear threshold); a complete lack of transport facilities for troops and equipment; and an absence of any ships suitable for action in the North Sea and the narrow waters. This is fairly serious for an island society with a trade pattern that remains 95 per cent maritime.

This is very different from the cry inspired by the Navy League, shouted up and down Whitehall in 1908: 'We want eight [dreadnoughts] and we won't wait.' But as a contribution to the debate it is to be welcomed. Taxpayers have a right to be heard, and even admirals pay income tax. The politician's difficulty, in government, is caused by the general lack of understanding of the purpose of a navy and of what the different components of that navy can be expected to do. This is coupled with widespread disagreement about the threat to the nation and the circumstances in which a future maritime war might be fought, as well as about the deterrent value of a navy. There are complicated arguments about cost and military effectiveness, as also about the separate but important consideration of what is now at the least a ten-year construction period. However rich a country may be, there must be a physical limit in peacetime (when a navy is built) to the capacity of the shipyards and factories, and to fill their books with the wrong kind of order makes it difficult, if not impossible, for future naval planners to change the navy's shape in a hurry, as experience has shown.

Thus it is because the problem has a respectable pedigree that we think it worthwhile to return to first principles by considering the origins of the modern navy by types of warship.

Chapter Two

BATTLESHIP

The British Battle-fleet is like the queen on the chessboard . . .
it is the final arbiter at sea; to lose it is to lose the game.
ADMIRAL OF THE FLEET LORD CHATFIELD,
First Sea Lord, 1933–8

At about four o'clock in the morning of 25 October 1944 the age of the battleship came to an end off the island of Leyte in the Philippines. In the Surigao Strait an American battle-fleet was waiting for the remnant of an approaching Japanese force, 16 miles away to the south. Vice-Admiral Shoji Nishimura had already lost the battleship *Fuso* to torpedo attack by American destroyers; he continued his northerly course in the battleship *Yamashiro*, now with only the cruiser *Mogami* and one destroyer in company.

Rear-Admiral Jesse B. Oldendorf had deployed a sizeable force of cruisers, destroyers and torpedo-boats to intercept, as well as the 'battle line' under the command of Rear-Admiral George L. Weyler. His six battleships were not the most powerful in the United States Navy, for all were more than twenty years old; and of the six, five had been damaged or sunk in the surprise attack on Pearl Harbor on the first day of the Pacific War. Not quite three years later, salvaged and repaired or rebuilt, these survivors, *West Virginia*, *Maryland*, *Tennessee*, *California* and *Pennsylvania*, formed the line of battle with *Mississippi*.

At seven minutes to four, when the range was 11 and a half miles, *West Virginia*'s radar-controlled 16-inch guns opened fire. *Tennessee* and *California* followed, then *Maryland*. At eight minutes past four *Mississippi* fired the very last big gun salvo that a battleship was to fire at her own kind. Eleven minutes later the huge *Yamashiro* rolled over and sank. There were few survivors.

The battleship, or line-of-battle ship as she was known in the days of sail, has had a long history. For more than four centuries she dominated naval warfare. The line-of-battle ship survived into the age of steam and shed her sails; massively armoured, mounting heavy artillery, she assumed her final shape in the battleship *Dreadnought* in the early years of the twentieth century. *Dreadnought* was the prototype of every one of the 150 huge dreadnought battleships that were to be built for the world's navies during the next forty years—all of the same basic design as *Dreadnought* herself. Of those 150, thirty were lost in the two world wars; four are laid up in reserve in United States Navy yards; and four others are preserved in the United States as museum pieces, state memorials. All the rest have long since been broken up for scrap. As we write, a vigorous debate has begun about reactivating two of the US Navy's reserve battleships for the deployment of large numbers of cruise missiles, so the battleship could still be seen in action again.

Throughout that forty-year period—spanning two world wars—the dreadnoughts were, in practice, the strategic deterrent of the day, as well as being the backbone of every navy of importance until well into the Second World War. Thereafter the battleship declined in significance, until a dozen years later she had all but vanished. Between the wars international treaties regulated the size of battleships and the number each state might possess, very much as the Strategic Arms Limitation Treaties seek to limit the strategic nuclear arsenals of the super-powers today.

1 Battle-fleet, 1914. Sea power was thought to depend on the outcome of the 'decisive encounter'.

The twentieth-century battleship, the dreadnought, was the most impressive weapons system of her time and certainly the most expensive. In her latest form each huge ship was a mobile, 45,000-ton floating fortress that could move at 30 miles an hour or more: each was 250 yards long, 36 yards wide, built around a battery of eight or nine super-heavy, long-range guns, all of the same calibre (usually 14-, 15- or 16-inch, though right at the end of the era the outsize Japanese battleships *Yamato* and *Musashi* carried enormous 18-inch pieces). The US Navy's 16-inch gun can hurl its projectile more than 20 miles. The huge, elongated shell is 1 and a quarter tons of steel, solid except for the 'bursting charge', a mere 40 pounds of high explosive. It was designed to punch a hole through armour-plate of toughened steel more than 1 foot thick on the deck or side of an enemy ship, before bursting inside her vital parts—machinery spaces or the magazines. The battleship's big guns could outrange and overwhelm any lesser warship, and because she was herself massively armoured, she could accept considerable damage, even from the guns of a similarly equipped enemy.

The battleship as a special sort of fighting ship emerged towards the end of the fifteenth century as a consequence of improvements in sailing-ship design in the period of the great voyages of discovery, and especially improvements in gunnery. For centuries before then naval warfare had closely resembled war on land. Opposing fleets were usually composed of oar-driven galleys, which would lie alongside each other, and storming parties of soldiers as well as sailors fought hand to hand, as if for possession of a castle. The faster sailing vessel gave the fleet a new kind of mobility: she could stand off to destroy or disable her enemy by gunfire alone. At first the new weapon of artillery had been imperfectly understood. Guns were small and mounted in the 'fore-castle' or the 'aftercastle'; they were intended to bring down the enemy's sail and rigging and to kill or wound his soldiers and sailors before the boarding party could storm over the side on to his deck and finish the job. As sail displaced oars, it became possible to mount a battery of heavier guns, whose great weight dictated that they be placed low down in the hull, muzzles pointing outboard on each side, replacing the galley's oarsmen. The warship now had a much enhanced destructive power, which was to be employed in destroying *ships* rather than *men*. This change in emphasis was to be repeated more than once in modern times. The fighting ship had emerged as a type distinct from the merchantman. An important safety measure was the introduction of gun ports—doors in the ship's side that could be closed on passage and in rough weather. In the first naval artillery duel between English and French fleets in 1545, in the Battle of the Azores in 1582 and in the Armada campaign of 1586–8 this new kind of naval warfare was being developed, and as it advanced, the oared galley was forced into the backwaters of Europe, the Mediterranean and the Baltic. With half his ship's heavy armament on each side, a captain might rake his opponents with a broadside, then turn about on the other tack of sail to close again, firing the guns on his previously disengaged side. The lengthy business of reloading could be undertaken at a safe distance from the enemy's small-arms fire.

2 Convoy, 1941. Sea power now meant the protection of merchant ships, not the clash of battle-fleets. Naval tactics were thus completely reversed.

The broadside was the means of delivering concentrated fire-power; and since these heavy pieces could not be pointed ahead or astern, the obvious formation for a squadron or even a fleet of ships was 'line ahead', each ship closely following her consort. Strict line discipline was essential to preserve the cohesion of the fleet; it permitted concentration of fire upon a part of the enemy; and when two opposing fleets joined battle, this formation allowed each captain to engage the nearest ship in the enemy's line. As early as the middle of the seventeenth century, line of battle had become official British tactical doctrine. Line-of-battle ships were rated according to their armament, a three-decker first-rate mounting about a hundred guns, a third-rate fifty.

An admiral would seek to gain the 'weather gage' by placing his fleet to windward of the enemy, thus securing the initiative; for, if successful, he could determine the range and the moment at which he would fight, while his opponent would find it hard to redeploy against the wind. The accepted doctrine was to deliver a crushing blow by the weight and rapidity of gunfire. The 32-pounder cannon, on the lowest gun deck, fired solid iron shot—the cannon-ball—to a distance of 1 mile and a half, but anything like accurate shooting was possible only at a quarter of a mile or even less (the distance the shot would travel horizontally). Almost all actions were fought at point-blank range—300 to 400 yards—and often much closer. In spite of official British insistence on keeping a rigid line of battle, the common outcome was a confused struggle—single-ship actions, in which in-dividual captains pounded away at each other until one ship was a blazing, dismasted wreck, with most of her sailors and marines dead. Surrender was not a disgrace to the loser of the heavy gun duel.

The first-rate ship of the line was small by twentieth-century standards—only about 2000 tons—but she needed a large crew to work the sails and fight the big guns. *Victory*, Nelson's flagship at Trafalgar, had a complement of more than 800, most of the seamen being forcibly enlisted by the press gang. French three-deckers of the time were usually half as large again in tonnage and in complement. The very last wooden-walled ships of the line, constructed in the 1860s, embodied the technological improvements of three centuries of naval gunnery: in the fifty years since Trafalgar the effective range of cannon had increased from 300 to 700 yards. These mid-Victorian battleships were very powerful weapons systems, but during the next twenty years they were driven from the line of battle by the new high-explosive shell. The wooden three-decker suddenly became so much firewood.

3 The last of the wooden-walls: the first-rate, three-decker, line-of-battle ship HMS Victoria (1859). 7000 tons, sixty muzzle-loaders each side, 12 knots under sail and slightly faster under steam.

Even while the last of them were building, new technology was changing the shape of modern navies. Already the two leading sea powers, Britain and France, possessed early steam-driven ships of the line, still with masts and yards for the spread of canvas that would be needed until the steam engine could be made reliable and until a worldwide chain of coaling stations would make feasible long voyages by steam. More powerful and more accurate guns were being developed; now an enemy ship might be destroyed at much longer range—a mile or more. To survive the high-explosive shell a warship needed armour, and in 1859 the first 'ironclad' appeared, the French *Gloire*, followed three years later by HMS *Warrior*, the first to be launched with an iron hull. (She is still afloat, the precursor of every steel battleship ever built.) Although she had to be officially classed as a third-rate line-of-battle ship, measured by complement, *Warrior* outclassed every first-rate in the wooden-walled sailing line of battle.

A triple technological revolution had begun: that of steam, guns and iron. The wooden-walled ships of the line gave place to vessels with a lower profile, as wood was replaced by iron for hull as well as armour-plating. The long rows of cannon on each side were replaced by fewer and heavier guns. In time, the guns would be mounted on the centre line in armoured turrets. As the steam engine proved more reliable, the yard-arms, rigging and sails vanished; masts would remain for *essential but secondary purposes only*, for gunnery control, lookouts and signalling. The great weight of an ironclad, armoured sailing ship would have required an enormous area of sail, and the tall masts, the yards and the spread of canvas would have made such a vessel dangerously unstable. Thus one technical advance hastened another.

Improvements in naval artillery went ahead at the same pace. The new breech-loading gun did not require hauling about the deck like a muzzle-loader, which had to be swabbed out and reloaded after its firing, then dragged back into its firing position. The rifled gun gave its projectile a spinning flight, straighter than that of the old cannon-ball; and, with the passing of the wooden-walled ship, that projectile had to pierce armour-plate. Here the gun met its match, for the first-ever duel between armoured ships, which took place during the American Civil War, was a victory for armour.

Despite these technical innovations, naval warfare changed little in the half-century that separated the first ironclads from *Dreadnought*. Naval gunnery was still far from being an exact science: each gun was layed and trained individually by the gun-layer, who had to be able to see his target plainly and to make his own allowance for roll, pitch and yaw, as well as for the moving target. Not surprisingly, shooting was often wildly inaccurate, even at point-blank range. Most naval officers still expected sea warfare to be much as it had been in the days of Nelson: the line of battle; a prolonged exchange of fire at close range (a mile or less); battleships leaving the line to attack with the strangest of new weapons, the ram; boarding parties fighting hand to hand with cutlass, pistol and pike (the pike survived in the Royal Navy until 1905, and the cutlass was used by Vian of the *Cossack*'s men when boarding the *Altmark* in 1940). Armour-plate might protect the battleship from mortal wounds, so emphasis was placed on the volume and rapidity of fire. In some respects, naval warfare had returned to an earlier age, as the steam engine made fleets independent of the wind, and warships regained the mobility of the oar-propelled galleys—albeit a vastly enhanced mobility. Marine engineering was developing fast. The reciprocating engine would eventually be replaced by the steam turbine, and this alone greatly extended a fleet's radius of action; before the steam turbine, first installed in *Dreadnought* (earlier in some smaller warships), a battleship could spend only about two or three days at sea before she had to return to harbour for maintenance.

4 Forty years on from HMS Victoria. One of the last pre-Dreadnought battleships, HMS Edward VII. Note the variety of armament—12-inch, 9·2-inch, 6-inch and many smaller guns.

The more or less simultaneous introduction of breech-loading, rifled artillery, the steam engine and armour-plate signalled the start of the modern naval armaments race. Each class of fighting ship constituted a challenge to other naval powers; a new French battleship would be answered a couple of years later by a more powerful British design. Armour-plate was made thicker, and toughened steel was used rather than iron, while guns grew larger, firing heavier shell to a greater range.

Battleships, as they came to be known from about 1880, were bigger, stronger, more destructive—and more expensive. The old wooden three-decker line-of-battle ship, some of which had more than 100 muzzle-loaders, had taken much longer to build, but she lasted fifty or sixty years without alteration, and she remained an effective weapons platform throughout her long life. The all-steel battleship, heavily armed and armoured, could be built very quickly (*Dreadnought* took a year) but also quickly became obsolete. The Royal Navy was now drawing heavily on the country's industrial base and its scientific resources—on the chemical industry for explosives, on the metallurgical industry for armour-plate and shells, on the electrical industry for early computers, lighting and ventilation, on heavy engineering for huge propulsion systems. In all these new fields the Royal Navy was working at the very frontiers of technology.

While the triple revolution of steam, guns and iron had given the battleship a new offensive power, almost at once the same high technology produced new defensive weapons. The under-water mine, usually moored and at first known as the 'torpedo', and its younger cousin, a self-propelled mine known as the 'locomotive' or 'fish' torpedo and invented in the 1860s, now threatened the battleship.

5 HMS Dreadnought *(1906). Ten 12-inch guns but only small-calibre weapons for defence against torpedo boats.* Dreadnought *made all existing battleships obsolete.*

Thenceforth armour-plate had to be provided in a protective belt above the waterline to stop shells and below it to withstand mine and torpedo; compartments were subdivided; coal and, later, oil fuel was used as shock-absorber; steel nets were hung from the battleship's side in harbour to catch torpedoes. The first torpedo-launching platform was the small, fast, nimble torpedo-boat. To counter this new threat, batteries of quick-firing guns and even machine-guns were mounted; the battleship's main armament was too unwieldy for this task. Screening the battle-fleet were the new torpedo-boat destroyers. For the first time admirals had to learn that their powerful modern battleships were at risk from what they thought of as insignificant little craft.

By the turn of the century the Royal Navy was still the world's largest, able to defeat any two naval powers combined (the so-called 'Two-Power Standard'). The challenge to British battleship strength had hitherto come from France and Russia, but in the United States and Germany the writings of an American naval officer, Alfred Thayer Mahan, had a profound influence. Mahan preached the primacy of the battle-fleet, upon which rested a nation's maritime security and power. The Imperial German navy had for thirty years been little more than a coast-defence force, but now it was to have a modern battle-fleet designed to fight in the North Sea. The challenge to the Royal Navy was obvious and serious. Although it might not be possible, or even desirable, to build a battle-fleet of equal size and strength, Germany was creating a 'risk fleet', one that would guarantee that a British naval victory would be too costly. In political terms, the Kaiser's battle-fleet policy failed; the threatened nation (Britain) moved closer to France, and the immediate technical effect was a quickening of the naval armaments race that had begun in the 1880s. This race became almost a stampede in 1906 when *Dreadnought* appeared, the first truly modern battleship, the all big-gun ship that naval architects had talked about for some half-dozen years, embodying several revolutions in design, propulsion, armament and fire control. *Dreadnought* was the model for almost every subsequent battleship. Indeed, she was more: so advanced was her design that every naval great power was obliged to demote its existing battle-fleet to reserve status and to build ships like her. Thenceforth these were all called 'dreadnoughts' to distinguish them from the pre-*Dreadnought* battleships.

Since *Dreadnought* was the first large warship to be propelled by steam turbines rather than reciprocating engines, she could stay at sea longer and steam faster than her predecessors. Speed was one of her important features; protection was another, through armour and watertight compartments. Earlier battleships mounted two, sometimes four, heavy guns up to 12-inch in calibre and a mixed armament of medium artillery. One American class carried 12-inch, 8-inch and 7-inch guns, and the eight British King Edward VII-class ships, completed at about the same time as *Dreadnought*, mounted four 12-inch guns, four 9·2-inch and ten 6-inch, with light artillery (for use against enemy torpedo-boats) of fourteen 12-pounders and fourteen 3-pounders. Even the two Lord Nelson-class ships, the last pre-*Dreadnought* battleships built for the Royal Navy which were completed in 1908, carried four 12-inch and ten 9·2-inch guns, with twenty-four 12-pounders. Each of these guns had different ballistics; their shells had a different trajectory and time of flight and widely varying ranges, so each separate calibre would have to be layed and trained to quite different angles to hit the same target. *Dreadnought* broke new ground with just one main battery of ten 12-inch guns and no secondary armament (except very small quick-firing guns to deal with torpedo-boats); she thus embodied a revolution in naval gunnery. In the hundred years since Trafalgar there had been very few naval battles, but it was generally expected that a modern sea fight would still take the form of a lengthy cannonade. Relatively small guns would demoralize the enemy with a hail of shells. In *Dreadnought* the Royal Navy proclaimed its faith, for the first time, in the much heavier shell, fired further by the big gun.

The second part of the gunnery revolution concerned fire control. Tsushima in 1905 was to be the last naval battle fought in the old-fashioned way, with each gun individually aimed by its gun-layer at a target selected by him. At a battle range of a mile or so such a method was wasteful of ammunition, even if the guns' crews were well trained, because the individual gun-layer could not be sure which were his own hits or misses. At the longer ranges now possible with the larger guns the difficulty was even greater. *Dreadnought*'s uniform heavy armament produced shell splashes close together, which made it easier to adjust the aim, and with it director firing—a form of centralized fire control—had arrived.

In future the gun-layer would not need to see his target; he would train and elevate his gun on instructions from the gunnery officer and the fire-control team, most of whom would not be able to see the target either. When *Dreadnought* was commissioned the Royal Navy's fire-control system was in the early stages of development, but director firing and a central calculating position below decks had been introduced in most battleships of the Grand Fleet by the time of Jutland ten years later; the complete fire-control system was perfected between the wars. It involved the gunnery officer (principal control officer) in the spotting-top, a control position on the foremast about 100 feet above the waterline, which afforded a good view clear of smoke, spray, haze and shell splashes; the director layer and the range-takers in the director-rangefinder position just above the spotting-top; the crew of the transmitting station (called the 'main battery plot' in the similar US Navy system) well below the waterline; and the guns' crews in the turrets.

The enemy's range was taken constantly and simultaneously by several rangefinders (in effect, huge double telescopes up to 30 feet long) and the mean computed; this and his estimated course and speed were passed down to the transmitting station. The time of flight of the shell, the temperature of the upper air, wind speed (long-range firing required a high angle of elevation), the ship's own course and speed, her roll, pitch and yaw—all these and much more were fed into calculating machines in the transmitting station, where a 'solution to the fire-control problem' was obtained. The appropriate angles of elevation and training were then passed to the guns. This use of calculating machines represents one of the earliest applications of the electromechanical computer. The complete system was only made possible by electricity at a time when, on shore, electricity was scarcely used even for lighting and was very rarely the energy source for industry. Long before the First World War electricity was being generated for lighting and power in all the ships of the fleet; for example, as early as the 1870s armoured ships were ventilated between decks by huge fans powered by electric motors. Mains electricity supplies were also needed for the gunnery fire-control circuits to indicate remotely, on dials at the big guns, the bearing and range for the gun-layers and trainers to follow, to display the state of readiness of the armament and, finally, to fire all the guns at once by remote control. In this way all the big guns could be aimed at the same target and fired together. This may seem normal, even simple, today, but at the turn of the century it was a remarkable technological break-through, hardly paralleled in any other field of engineering. Director firing produced both uniformity and concentration of fire: with only one battery of at least six or eight identical guns, a full broadside (or salvo, using only half the guns) enabled the gunnery officer to correct his aim quickly by observing the fall of shot, which might be 'over' or 'short', left or right. Even so, very few projectiles would ever reach their target; in action perhaps no more than three in a hundred heavy shells would score a hit, although this depended as much on the skill of the gunnery officer and his team as on the quality of his equipment.

The early twentieth-century battleship already resembled the heavy industrial plant of the future. The shells, weighing between 800 pounds and 1 ton or more, were delivered to the guns by hydraulic or electric hoists, as were the cartridges to expel the shell from the gun—four, sometimes six, silken bags of cordite (nitro-glycerine and tri-nitrocellulose, extruded in long, thin sticks) brought up from the magazine 50 feet below. A well trained turret's crew could load, fire, reload and fire the huge main armament guns again in one minute.

British naval officers of this era had been schooled in the traditions of Nelson and the other great admirals of the age of sail. They had been taught the virtues of the offensive, much as officers of the French army were in 1870 and 1914. They were not particularly encouraged to read naval and military history, which might have enlarged their view. From the First Sea Lord downwards, it was held as an article of faith that since the Royal Navy was a fighting service, designed for combat, it should seek an encounter with the enemy immediately on the outbreak of war with the aim of destroying his battle-fleet.

For a dozen years the British had been trained and equipped to fight that decisive battle with the German fleet when war came, as it surely must. In 1914 British officers were still supremely confident of victory, given their superiority in numbers of dreadnoughts (twenty-one to thirteen), and they had no doubt that after they had won this battle the enemy's lesser warships would be picked off at leisure. Few officers considered the possibility that the weaker German fleet would sensibly refuse to fight. It was as well, perhaps, for the Royal Navy that the Germans did not give battle early in the war, because the British margin of superiority was then narrowed by mechanical failure in some ships and by the sinking of the dreadnought

Audacious, which struck a mine. (Her loss was kept secret until after the war.) Besides, the Grand Fleet needed the twenty-one months' respite before Jutland to train and work up to an acceptable standard of shooting.

The prevailing view in the Service that only a decisive fleet action could give the Royal Navy command of the sea quite overlooked the reality that the Royal Navy already exercised general, worldwide command of the sea. From the start of the war nearly all of the German navy and almost all the then large German merchant marine had been denied the use of the sea by the British blockade except in the Baltic, and even there it was harried by British submarines. Few British naval officers, and hardly any of the British public, understood that the Grand Fleet was best employed not in fighting but in being poised to do so—a massive deterrent of the kind familiar enough in a later, nuclear age. The decisive battles would be fought on land, for the battle-fleet could not win a war. Its Commander-in-Chief, Sir John Jellicoe, knew that his battleships were vulnerable to underwater damage from mine and torpedo, so he was afraid to risk his ships in the southern parts of the North Sea or near the German bases. He possessed an immensely powerful but inflexible instrument, to which it is not fanciful to compare today's strategic nuclear forces. His tactical unit was not the battle*ship*, but the battle-*fleet*. At Jutland Jellicoe's Grand Fleet was divided into three battle squadrons, each squadron subdivided into two divisions of four battleships each—twenty-four battleships in all, with six admirals, as well as Jellicoe in the fleet flagship, *Iron Duke*. Yet, in keeping with custom, command of this colossal armada was rigidly centralized. Each battleship was required to keep station exactly 500 yards astern of her next ahead. The fleet would cruise in six columns, and when the enemy fleet was sighted, the columns would be deployed into one battle line some 6 miles in length. The aim was to deploy the line at right angles to the enemy's line of advance while he was still in cruising formation, in columns; this made possible a concentration of fire upon the leading enemy ships, while the enemy could not bring all of his guns to bear. The manoeuvre, seldom achieved in battle, was called 'crossing the T' of the enemy.

The battle-fleet did not fight alone. It was screened at a distance by light cruisers, whose task was to locate the enemy fleet, to report to the Commander-in-Chief and, if possible, to draw the enemy battle-fleet within range of the guns of the Grand Fleet. This scouting force was stiffened by a new kind of ship, the battle-cruiser, large, fast, heavily gunned but lightly armoured, and intended to overwhelm the enemy's light cruisers. In the opening stage of the Battle of Jutland British and German battle-cruisers fought each other, and in this heavy-weight skirmishing the larger British force came off second-best.

The Battle of Jutland was certainly on a grand scale: in all, 250 warships and 100,000 men, British and German, took part. On the following day nearly 9000 were dead. But Jutland was not the decisive encounter of battle-fleets that the Royal Navy had expected from the very first day of war, an encounter which the numerically inferior High Seas Fleet had until then refused. The German battle-cruisers had made occasional forays into the North Sea and had even bombarded coastal towns in north-east England; but in May 1916 they were deployed as bait to lure Vice-Admiral Beatty's battle-cruisers to destruction by the waiting High Seas Fleet and to entice the Grand Fleet into a submarine ambush. Thus on each side the battle-cruisers were supported at a distance by a slower but very much more powerful battle-fleet, though only the British Commander-in-Chief was seeking a fleet action.

When the long awaited clash came, it was to some extent a surprise to both sides: although each was vaguely aware of the other's activity through listening to enemy wireless messages, the opposing battle-cruisers stumbled into each other. Even so, more than two hours passed before Sir John Jellicoe learned of the presence not only of the enemy's reconnaissance force but also of his battle-fleet; while in turn Admiral Scheer blindly led his dreadnoughts into a crescent of fire from Jellicoe's twenty-four battleships in line, which battered Scheer's leading ships. Twice that evening, in the failing light, Jellicoe 'crossed the T' of his opponent, and twice Scheer skilfully disengaged in a well rehearsed manoeuvre. Most of the heavy ships were coal-burners, and in the smoke and the gathering gloom visibility was poor. Radar was a quarter of a century away. The battleships of the Grand Fleet mounted bigger guns firing heavier shell, and for the short time they were in action their shooting, at a range of 6 miles or more, was good. But not one dreadnought battleship was sunk on either side on this one and only occasion on which the doctrine of the modern dreadnought battle-fleet was to be put to the test, for there was nothing remotely resembling

Jutland in the Second World War. That night the retreating Germans passed very close to the Grand Fleet but were not challenged or even reported, let alone fired on; only the light forces clashed.

By a simple tally of ships lost, Jutland was a German victory; but the British casualties, though grievous, were borne by the auxiliary forces of battle-cruisers, cruisers and destroyers. The British battle-fleet remained intact and ready to fight again; the battered German fleet had retreated to its base, leaving Britain still in command of the seas. Paradoxically, had the High Seas Fleet stayed for further battle—and almost certain annihilation—the war would probably not have ended one day sooner. Jellicoe could only have triumphed at some cost to himself, and for the surviving battleships of the Grand Fleet to attempt offensive operations off the German coast, defended as it was by U-boats, minefields and coastal artillery, would have been hazardous and pointless. The British naval blockade continued as before, maintained by the distant cruisers; and there was little more the Royal Navy could reasonably be expected to do, save to defend Britain's maritime commerce against a German counter-blockade and to guard the communications of the now sizeable British army fighting the enemy in France.

If his opponent very sensibly refused battle on unfavourable terms, Jellicoe and his successor, Sir David Beatty, who had previously commanded the battle-cruisers, were also cautious. It was said of Jellicoe that he was the only man on either side who could lose the war in an afternoon. This was, of course, a colourful exaggeration, but to the end the Grand Fleet, the most powerful single force of battleships the world had ever seen, the 'fleet in being', was conserved. At the outbreak of war there had been twenty-one British dreadnoughts to Germany's thirteen; at Jutland, twenty-eight to sixteen; and at the war's end, there were twenty-nine British (and five American) to nineteen German dreadnoughts.

The failure of the British and German battle-fleets to fight it out, and the inconclusive nature of their one encounter, did not shake either professional or public confidence in the battleship. At the Armistice the Admiralty insisted that the German battle-fleet be interned under British guard until its disposal could be agreed by the victorious powers—though most of the big ships were eventually scuttled by their crews in Scapa Flow. Although

Britain was still the world's greatest naval power, many of her ships were in need of replacement after a long war. The 'Two-Power Standard' had been abandoned; Britain would henceforth attempt only to match any one naval power. Her new rivals were the United States and Japan.

All three nations had ambitious building programmes, and all had begun work on yet larger and more powerful battleships. The absurdity of a new naval armaments race among allies, just after the 'war to end wars', was manifest. Fortunately for Britain, whose economy had been seriously weakened by the war, the extra financial burden was avoided by unanimous acceptance of the Washington Naval Treaty in 1922. The Treaty set limits to fleets and to the size of each type of warship. The battleship was not to exceed 35,000 tons displacement, and much new construction was halted, while such new ships as were permitted had to have a life of twenty years before replacement. The United States, Britain and Japan were allocated a tonnage in the proportions 5:5:3 respectively. We might note in passing that after the abrogation of the Treaty new battleships were much bigger; *Bismarck*, for example, exceeded 50,000 tons, and the last two built by the Japanese nearer 70,000. These arms limitation talks and the subsequent Treaty reflected the maritime interests of the world powers, the USA, Britain and Japan, with France and Italy, the five signatories. Germany was defeated and was allowed only a small navy for coast defence; the Soviet Union was exhausted and ostracized; of the victors, the United States and Britain had small armies and large navies. The Washington Treaty was thus largely an understanding between two potential rivals at sea, with a third party, Japan, closely interested. Although it makes strange reading today, American admirals then undoubtedly thought of Britain as a commercial rival who might well become a naval opponent. Until the resurgence of Germany the war plans of the United States were shaped by the likelihood of war on two fronts, with an Asian enemy (Japan) and a European enemy (Britain), at the same time: hence the concern expressed by her admirals in the 1920s at the apparent superiority of the Royal Navy in terms of numbers of ships and material—for example, British battleships could elevate their guns to 30 degrees against the Americans' 20 degrees, giving the British much greater range. The big gun was still the chief weapon, and the battleship was still regarded as the chief weapons system, the tactical unit remaining, as before, the battle-fleet. The rest of any navy of consequence was still to be organized around it.

The battleship and the battle-fleet thus remained the heart of the navy, and the submarine and the aircraft were still thought of as auxiliaries. From the 1920s the battleship was fitted with more smaller-calibre weapons with a high angle of elevation to engage enemy aircraft. Against the very low-flying aircraft and the near-vertical approach of the dive-bomber, heavy machine-guns and 'cannon', such as the Bofors 40mm and the 2-pounder pom-pom in multiple moutings, were widely fitted in the US Navy and the Royal Navy.

The battleship designer's task was made more difficult by these new requirements. Quick-firing weapons consume a staggering amount of ammunition, which requires its own ready-use lockers and shell-rooms; and although the smaller-calibre ammunition was safer, being 'fixed' (shell and cartridge together, instead of the heavy gun's cordite charges, which were kept in a separate magazine) more shell-rooms and magazines made for less protection, as the armoured 'citadel' was pierced by additional trunks and hatches for ammunition supply. Ideally, the battleship should have been able to leave her protection to the screen of lighter craft and to interceptor aircraft and, of course, to her own passive defences of armour, speed and manoeuvrability, as well as the subdivision of internal compartments and a vigorous damage-control and fire-fighting organization. However, few sailors would accept such a radical policy, and as the Second World War progressed, more and more light anti-aircraft weapons were mounted in battleships, until it became apparent that against a determined—and sometimes suicidal—airman, the comparatively light 20mm and 40mm shells were not enough, even if they did sometimes hit an attacking aircraft. As was the case with the torpedo-boats and torpedo-carrying destroyers, so it was with an aircraft: a much heavier projectile was needed to destroy an attacker, and this required a larger gun with a correspondingly slower rate of fire. In the final six months of the Pacific War, battleships being refitted were losing some of their 20mm guns that had so recently been added, and because of their size and stability they became the best platforms for heavy anti-aircraft batteries. They even suffered the indignity of being used in this role to protect the aircraft-carriers that had supplanted them as the heart of the fleet.

Before this situation arose, and between the wars, navies and air forces hotly disputed the claims of the bomber and the battleship. Airmen confidently asserted that the battleship was an easy prey for bombing aircraft, but tests carried out by the Americans and the British on surrendered German dreadnoughts were inconclusive, the results appearing to confirm the prejudices of both airmen and sailors. The admirals noted how difficult it was to sink a modern heavily armoured battleship by bombs. Air-launched torpedoes proved a greater threat in British fleet exercises in the 1920s, but the Admiralty discounted the lesson. Torpedo-carrying aircraft were intended, it believed, only to slow down an enemy fleet, to bring it to action in a big-gun battle, perhaps because the gunnery specialist was still dominant over the other branches of the naval service. The 'big-gun club' ruled in the British, American and Japanese navies. The Battle of Jutland was fought again and again in every naval war college.

By 1939 the battleship had reached her final shape and size as a result of the designers' efforts to meet the requirements of hitting power, speed and protection. The weight of armour on gun turrets, barbettes, decks and the ship's side (which accounted for as much as one-third of the ship's tonnage), and the weight of the increasingly elaborate fire-control positions high above the waterline, created instability which had to be corrected by giving the ship a deep draught and a broad beam. This necessitated a greater length of hull to accommodate the more powerful main engines required to drive a larger vessel at high speed, and this led in turn to much greater fuel stowage. Ever since the appearance of *Dreadnought* herself, speed had been valued as highly as fire-power and protection. The fast battleship had shown her worth at Jutland, where the slower ships of the Grand Fleet had been unable to deploy fast enough for battle or to overhaul a retreating enemy. Designers endeavoured to economize on weight and space by packing two, three, even four heavy guns into the one turret and by specifying a general-purpose secondary armament, as in the King George V-class 5·25-inch or the Americans' 5-inch gun. (The Germans gave *Bismarck* and *Tirpitz* a separate anti-aircraft battery, one of several surprisingly old-fashioned features of their design.) Limits to draught, beam and length were imposed by the size of existing dry docks and by the width and depth of harbour channels and waterways such as the Panama Canal; to the very end of the battleship era the American ships had to be able to redeploy rapidly from the Atlantic Ocean to the Pacific, avoiding the long passage round the Horn or the Cape of Good Hope.

In *Vanguard*, the last of the third generation of British dreadnoughts, her designers finally got it right: she was universally regarded as one of the best dreadnought battleships of them all. A far better sea boat than the comparable American Iowa class, she rolled less in a heavy sea and shipped less green water over her decks. It is ironical that by the time she could demonstrate these qualities, the idea of the battleship, the mobile, floating, armoured heavy-gun platform, belonged to a bygone age.

Battleships have always required large crews, as would be expected for such huge weapons of war. *Dreadnought* had a crew of about 800—no more than Nelson's flagship *Victory*—though 2000 was modest for some Second World War battleships, as weapons and equipment became more complicated. As populous as a small town, the battleship of the 1930s and 1940s was a good deal busier, with much activity along her many miles of crowded steel streets. The town squares were called 'flats', small, fairly open areas off which led other passages and compartments. Every few yards a steel door closed behind the traveller, a hatch fastened above a ladder, as protection against fire, smoke and flooding. All trades and skills were practised in this community. The largest group, of course, was the seamen, practising their age-old craft of 'working' the ship—her anchors and cables, wire hawsers and great ropes, the many boats under power or oars and sail, the booms and ladders, the snow-white decks, the spit and polish. Their fighting job was to man the armament, big guns and smaller, and torpedoes, and they also doubled as electricians and telephone operators. They were nearly matched in numbers by the stokers (no longer shovelling coal now that oil-fired steam turbines powered the battleship), who manned the main and auxiliary machinery whose skilled maintenance fell to the socially superior engine-room artificers, graded from fifth-class to 'chief'. Then the office workers in this town, the writers and stores assistants, the sick-berth attendants, the 'regulating branch' (ship's police), the ordnance and electrical artificers. Each of these had his role to play in peace and war, but with more than a single ship involved the communicators formed an essential group. Visual communications were the province of the signalmen ('bunting-tossers'), who, under their Chief Yeoman of Signals, hoisted flags in code combinations and read flag signals; they flashed messages in morse code on a signal projector—in effect, a small searchlight—or on a hand-held 'Aldis' lamp, or a big, 20-inch searchlight; and at close quarters they also signalled with semaphore flags. Theirs was an open-air life, in contrast to the world of the wireless telegraphy office below. Close to the telegraphists were the coders; the more secret messages were encyphered and decyphered by officers.

Battleship society (at least until a major reorganization in 1956) remained a microcosm of life in Victorian or Edwardian England. A kind of 'upstairs, downstairs' world it must have appeared to the outsider, a society ranging downwards from the officers' messes to the bottom of the ladder on the seamen's and stokers' mess-decks. To the stranger the captain seemed indeed a distant monarch, in rank equal to an army brigadier. He ruled through 'the Bloke'—usually a commander, Royal Navy, with three gold rings on his sleeve—who was the ship's executive officer as well as second in command. It was the commander who ordered the ship's routine; he was the court of summary justice, although more serious offences against good order and naval discipline were dealt with by the captain. Seamanship matters were attended to by a (usually non-specialist) lieutenant-commander, called the first lieutenant; other Executive (now known as Seaman) Branch officers of lieutenant-commander's rank headed specialist departments—Gunnery, Torpedoes, Signals, Navigation; they would be known to each other as 'Guns', 'Torps', 'Flags' and 'Pilot'. Commander (E), with purple between his gold lace to denote his branch, was responsible for the engine-rooms, boiler-rooms and auxiliary machinery; he was assisted by other engineer officers. Other departments included the instructor lieutenant ('Schoolie'), with blue inside his gold lace, who mostly taught the midshipmen; the medical officer (red), normally a surgeon-commander or surgeon-lieutenant-commander; the dental surgeon ('Toothie') (orange); the paymaster ('Pusser') (white), of the Supply and Secretariat Branch. Here too was the chaplain. Beneath these exalted ranks were the rest of the wardroom: watchkeeping lieutenants of the Executive Branch, some of them already junior specialists in gunnery, torpedoes or signals, and one or more senior sub-lieutenants. In the warrant officers' mess, all having had many years' service on the lower deck, were the commissioned gunner, the commissioned gunner (T) (for torpedoes), the commissioned shipwright, the commissioned bo'sun, the commissioned engineers, the commissioned stores officers and the 'sparker bosun', the commissioned telegraphist. In the gunroom would be found the midshipmen and younger sub-lieutenants.

At the pinnacle of the 'downstairs' world stood the master-at-arms, in charge of the ship's police and, as senior rating in the ship, the only one to wear a frock coat and carry a sword when attired in ceremonial dress. Chief petty officers, chief engine-room artificers and chief stokers had separate messes, as did the petty officers, stoker petty officers and artificers.

Each junior ratings' 'broadside' mess (so called because in the days of sail the seamen lived behind the broadside guns) was ruled by a leading hand—leading seaman, leading stoker, leading telegraphist. Mess-decks were crowded, especially when war brought several new tradesmen—radio direction-finding and monitoring personnel, radar operators and plotters, radar mechanics, seaman anti-aircraft gunners and more, all slinging their personal hammocks where they could. Each mess catered for itself, two 'cooks' taking the meal to the ship's galley for roasting or stewing. 'Canteen messing' allowed each mess to contribute more to the official messing allowance if they wanted better food; but many of the old sweats preferred to eat frugally and to share the 'mess savings'. Even when 'general messing' was introduced in big ships, 'canteen messing' prevailed in destroyers and small craft for many more years.

Battleship routine was formal. At sea or in harbour each ship paid her respects to her seniors, this being determined by the captains' seniority in the Navy List. A battleship's captain would usually be senior to most commanding officers of smaller ships, and there was much piping and sounding of bugles, with officers and ratings standing to attention on the upper deck, as another ship passed or when the captain of another ship came over the side to be received with the honours appropriate to his rank. On Sunday the ship's company paraded on deck for 'Church' and 'Divisions', each division of about fifty men under their divisional officer, who was expected to know his seamen or stokers as a platoon commander knows his riflemen. There was the daily ceremony of 'Commander's Requestmen and Defaulters' and once a week the similar but even more imposing ritual over which the captain himself presided. Occasionally the order would be given to 'Clear lower deck', when the assembled ship's company, smartly removing headgear at the command 'Off caps', listened to any specially important announcement, or the monthly recital of the Articles of War, or judgment read on some sailor who had committed one of the more heinous offences requiring punishment to be awarded by the captain (in the gravest cases, approved by his admiral). The captain, flanked by his officers, would read the warrant, and the defaulter, standing between two of the ship's police, would listen impassively, while several hundred men fidgeted. Few of them would have known the defaulter, so vast was their floating barracks, and if sentenced to imprisonment—usually served in a detention barracks onshore—the man might well be drafted to another ship afterwards. Naval discipline was summary and strict.

The battleship was continually being painted and scrubbed and polished, her guns cleaned, her boats and cordage maintained. 'Commander's Rounds', and on Saturday mornings 'Captain's Rounds', were occasions prepared for with much scrubbing of mess tables and polishing of brass work. Preceded by a marine bugler sounding a long G, the great man would stride briskly along corridors and through flats and on to mess-decks, pausing often to run a white-gloved finger-tip along a shelf or sill. If the glove became soiled, the commander turned to the first lieutenant, who turned to the divisional officer, who turned to the master-at-arms, who turned to the petty officer, who turned to the leading hand for an explanation.

Every night in harbour the ancient ceremony of 'Rounds' took place: authority, usually commander, first lieutenant or officer of the day, marched through the mess-decks, escorted by the master-at-arms and his retinue, while men relaxing off-watch stiffened to attention as the little party clattered by. Strict discipline was, of course, necessary if accidents were to be avoided, but the formality of a big ship contrasted oddly with the quieter, though equally firm discipline of smaller ships. All warship life was monastic. No woman ever spent the night on board or even sailed in a ship; in those days ladies were permitted to come aboard only as officers' guests at dinner or at a reception in foreign ports. Sport was officially encouraged. Football matches were organized onshore; water-polo was played in harbour; there were pulling and sailing regattas; boxing was considered important. It was mainly through such sporting events that the sailors and marines got to know the inhabitants of the other streets in their floating town.

Officers were separated from the lower deck by a wide difference in education and social background, yet there were few ships—even among the biggest—in which this gulf was not bridged by genuine feelings of mutual respect. Professional skills and the obvious equality of risk were powerful unifying forces. The battleship carried no passengers. The humblest member of the ship's company had some essential task to perform; both he and his captain had an equal chance of drowning and thus an equal interest in sinking the enemy. To the outsider who noted the formality of battleship life, the easy, unstrained relationship of officers and men was the more remarkable.

In a squadron of two battleships or more, one vessel wore the flag of the admiral commanding the force. The admiral's bridge was quite separate from the captain's bridge, and each had his own communications staff. The admiral's staff also included specialist officers with responsibility for gunnery, torpedoes, signals, navigation and other functions of the squadron. A paymaster captain served as admiral's secretary. The Royal Navy had come late to the idea of a staff, and even by the Second World War an admiral afloat was not as well served as his equivalent, an army divisional commander, onshore. Ever since the introduction of wireless telegraphy, the Admiralty, unlike the War Office and the Air Ministry, had exercised direct operational control not only over fleets but also over squadrons and, on occasion, individual ships, sometimes even bypassing the force commander. This was for very good reasons, because the admiral at sea was often obliged to keep wireless silence lest he give away his position to the listening enemy, and so he could not easily co-ordinate activity beyond his own horizon. For intelligence and for a strategic view he was bound to be at a disadvantage by comparison with his superiors on shore, who could more effectively enlist the support of the other Services (for example, to order reconnaissance or strike by long-range shore-based aircraft). Headquarters staffs also had access to intelligence gleaned from their monitoring and decoding of the enemy's signals traffic, and they could maintain a two-way flow of information, as the admiral afloat could not. Besides, naval warfare was becoming more complicated. Aircraft, submarines and supporting forces far away might all become involved in the battle; it could only be directed sensibly from ashore. When wireless telegraphy went to sea senior officers afloat lost much of their freedom of action—and none of them liked it.

In the 1930s both British and French navies recognized that the battleship might well have to give chase to the enemy commerce-raider, the heavy cruiser or 'pocket battleship', in order to destroy her by gunfire before she could escape, but most naval planners still expected combat on the lines of Jutland or as similar as could be attained with the much smaller battle-fleets that were a consequence of the Washington Naval Treaty. Certainly, a major fleet action was expected in the Pacific by American and Japanese admirals alike. The British expected to fight such a battle in the Far East against the Japanese and in the Mediterranean against the Italian fleet.

Most of the world's surviving battleships had been modernized, some battle-cruisers having been converted to 'fast battleships' with better protection, and by 1937, with the expiry of the Washington Treaty, new battleships—third-generation dreadnoughts—were under construction in all the larger maritime countries. The United States, Britain and France agreed among themselves to raise the 35,000-ton limit to 45,000 tons, but already the Japanese had started work on two much larger ships, those of the Yamato class. The Anglo-German Naval Treaty of 1935 merely acknowledged that Germany had already begun the long-prepared rebuilding of a big-ship navy. The great 50,000-ton battleships *Bismarck* and *Tirpitz* (which were actually completed some years later) would have been followed by six more as part of a large but balanced fleet of heavy cruisers, battle-cruisers and lighter warships, but the six-year Z Plan was made on the assumption that war with Britain would not come until 1945. Japan entered the war with nine battleships and a battle-cruiser, with two battleships building. The Italian navy dominated the central Mediterranean with four battleships, soon to be joined by two more. On the outbreak of war the Royal Navy's battleship strength was twelve, of which all but two, *Nelson* and *Rodney*, were of First World War construction or earlier; the three battle-cruisers, and indeed most of the battleships, were no match for new ships like *Bismarck*. Five new ships of the King George V class were building.

Germany, having started her new construction programme too late, entered the Second World War with a very small big-ship navy, amounting to two powerful, well protected battle-cruisers, *Scharnhorst* and *Gneisenau*, and three armoured cruisers, the 'pocket battleships'. When the first of her third-generation dreadnought battleships, *Bismarck*, appeared in the

second year of war (with another, *Tirpitz*, building) the Royal
Navy's battleship strength began to seem insufficient to contain
them all in home and distant waters—a very different state of
affairs from that of the Grand Fleet in the previous conflict.
Battleships were now no longer expected to fight in large fleets in
the North Sea, with their base close by. The new battle zone was
the broad Atlantic and even beyond. Germany's few heavy ships
would be employed singly or in pairs as long-range commerce
raiders of such power that only battleships could overcome
them. Whenever one of these great warships—battleship, battle-
cruiser, heavy cruiser, 'pocket battleship'—was out in the
Atlantic, supported by oil tankers at pre-arranged points in the
ocean, Allied merchant shipping was at fearful risk. Like her U-
boat partner in the early years of the Second World War, the
commerce-raiding cruiser, or battle-cruiser, for preference
attacked ships *not* in convoy. Many convoys—especially troop
convoys—required British battleships in their escorts.

In the earlier conflict the Grand Fleet had made frequent
'sweeps' in the North Sea and had sallied out to intercept the
High Seas Fleet on its rare sorties, but from 1939 onwards the
Home Fleet and other battleship forces spent much more time at
sea, with consequent strain and wear on machinery. In the
1914–18 war the old High Seas Fleet had never tried to break out
of the North Sea past the long natural barrier of the British Isles,
but in both wars commerce raiders could and did evade the
patrolling cruisers to reach the Atlantic, there to vanish in the
wastes of ocean and to reappear in some shipping lane. Even
with long-range aircraft and radar, the Royal Navy found it hard
to detect the commerce raider, whether she was going out to her
hunting-ground, at large or returning home. Commerce raiding
by auxiliary cruisers was successful against merchantmen when
they were not in convoy, but though Germany's fleet of heavy
ships was small in number, it posed a serious threat that could be
contained only by a strong British battle squadron on continual
alert.

In May 1941, almost a year after the fall of France and more
than six months before the United States entered the war,
Bismarck headed into the North Atlantic accompanied by the
heavy cruiser *Prinz Eugen*, while five fuel tankers and two supply
ships sailed in support. *Bismarck* was intended to draw off the
battleship escort from the important convoys, so that *Prinz
Eugen* could attack them. Admiral Tovey, Commander-in-

Chief, Home Fleet, quickly learned that the German squadron was out, and soon his own cruisers made contact in the Denmark Strait, between Iceland and Greenland. In all some fifty British warships were involved in the hunt: five battleships, three battle-cruisers and two aircraft-carriers, together with cruisers and destroyers. First to join battle was Admiral Holland in the elderly battle-cruiser *Hood*, with the new battleship *Prince of Wales* in company. Neither ship was fully efficient—*Hood* lacked full armour protection and was unmodernized, while *Prince of Wales* had not yet worked up to a proper fighting state—unlike those of the enemy, who had carefully prepared for this sortie.

Perhaps because he was anxious to catch *Bismarck* before she disappeared again in the flurries of snow, the British admiral had to attack head-on, so that only half his main armament could bear on the enemy, who himself could train his full broadside on *Hood*, 'crossing the T'. After eight minutes *Hood* blew up, most probably because a shell had penetrated one of her magazines. More than 1400 men were lost, and only three survived. *Prince of Wales* was then subjected to a heavy concentration of fire, which damaged her seriously; with half her main armament defective, she broke off the action, but not before she had scored a vital hit on *Bismarck*, causing a fuel leak that meant the German sortie had to be abandoned. Admiral Lutjens decided to make for a French port. Tovey determined to prevent him from escaping, and an exciting chase followed half-way across the Atlantic, with *Bismarck* shadowed by cruisers and aircraft, while Fleet Air Arm torpedo-bombers scored a crippling hit on her rudder; she was then brought to action by the battleships *King George V* and *Rodney*. These pounded her into a flaming wreck in the space of just over an hour, but still she would not sink until torpedoes and her own scuttling charges completed her destruction. There were few survivors.

Against Britain's two other enemies some kind of fleet action had been expected, though in the event it was never with more than three battleships on either side. The Italian navy refused battle at the start of hostilities in 1940, and the intended fleet action became a chase, but the elderly British battleships were not fast enough to bring the enemy to action. A year later the one Italian battleship present escaped the trap sprung at Cape Matapan, when Admiral Cunningham's three battleships, using radar, surprised the enemy's cruisers at night, blowing them out of the water at very close range. Battleships were now no longer fighting only their own kind; already, in the second battle of Narvik, the battleship *Warspite* had destroyed eight large German destroyers in the fjords during the brief Norwegian campaign of 1940.

6 *USS* Missouri *bombarding the North Korean coast, 1950. The ultimate in battleship design, but she arrived too late. The* Iowa *class of fast battleship (1943) was already subordinate to the aircraft-carrier.*

In the war with Japan the Royal Navy did not, after all, have to fight the expected rearguard action against a superior battle-fleet. The Admiralty had originally planned to send seven battleships and battle-cruisers to the Indian Ocean, but when hostilities seemed imminent, after two years of war, British battleship strength was low. It was hoped that the dispatch to Far Eastern waters of just two large ships—the new battleship *Prince of Wales* and the elderly battle-cruiser *Repulse*—would have a deterrent effect on the Japanese command, just as the

German battleship *Tirpitz* exercised a profound influence over the British Home Fleet. It was not to be. The British admiral, Sir Tom Phillips, sailed to intercept Japanese troop transports off the Malayan coast, but both his big ships were swiftly overwhelmed by torpedo-carrying aircraft and bombers of the Japanese shore-based naval air force, large twin-engined machines flying from airfields near Saigon, some 400 miles away across the South China Sea. The bombers scored only two hits, but *Prince of Wales* was hit by six torpedoes and *Repulse* by five, and both sank with the loss of 900 lives. Admiral Phillips went down with his flagship. Three days before and half an ocean away, at Pearl Harbor, a far greater defeat had been suffered by the US Navy. Of its eight battleships at Pearl Harbor, seven were sunk or badly damaged; the eighth, in dry dock, sustained slight damage. The surprise attack was made—in peacetime— by a large force of Japanese bomber and torpedo aircraft.

This was the nadir in the long history of the battleship. A few weeks earlier *Barham* had been torpedoed by a U-boat in the eastern Mediterranean and had blown up and sunk with very heavy loss of life. Only days after the disaster at Pearl Harbor and the annihilation of Admiral Phillips's squadron in the South China Sea, *Queen Elizabeth* and *Valiant* were to be immobilized for many months by limpet mines from Italian midget submarines that had penetrated the Alexandria base. A sister ship, *Warspite*, had been severely damaged by bombs off Crete. In just over two years of war the Royal Navy had lost three battleships and two battle-cruisers—but only one of these to gunfire. For the first time in centuries the British Mediterranean Fleet was now without a single battleship, but rather than asking for replacements, the Commander-in-Chief, Admiral Cunningham, called instead for 'adequate and suitable air-striking power'—by which he meant shore-based aircraft.

Japan now had ten battleships and one battle-cruiser (the other three had been rebuilt as 'fast battleships'); the US Navy still had nine undamaged battleships, but only two of these were 'new construction', though eight more were building. The destruction of the American battle-fleet at Pearl Harbor had overturned the balance of naval power in the Pacific, though, as the war progressed, the absence of that battle-fleet made little difference to the course it took. Only once in the Pacific War did battleships fight their own kind, and this solitary battle-fleet action was a fitting sequel to the disaster at Pearl Harbor. Only two of the stricken American battle-fleet had been a total loss. Salvaged and repaired, the remaining six ships had rejoined the fleet. Nearly three years later five of those survivors were in a squadron of six battleships in the Leyte Gulf. In the battle of the Surigao Strait Rear-Admiral Weyler succeeded in 'crossing the T' of the Japanese admiral, himself now reduced to one battleship. Admiral Nishimura's flagship, the mighty *Yama-shiro*, was quickly sunk, the last battleship to be defeated by her own kind. It was also the last time that battleships would fight in line of battle; the action in the Surigao Strait thus marked the end of a tactical formation that had lasted for three centuries.

The primary tasks of the battleship were now those of anti-aircraft ship—fortuitously, as battleships had been armed, since Pearl Harbor, with a mass of heavy, remote-controlled, automatic cannon for their own survival—and of the coast-bombardment ship, a duty once thought the least important for a battle-fleet and for which simple, slow, unprotected, shallow-draught 'monitors' had long been specially built. Indeed, both tasks could now usually be performed better by naval aviation, with interceptor aircraft to destroy enemy bombers, and tactical bombers with a range well beyond the 15–20 miles the battleship's big guns could reach. Thus the ship that was to carry the aircraft for both these tasks now displaced the battleship as the heart of every modern navy.

The battleship had a long reign as the very epitome of sea power, as the most formidable and technologically advanced weapons system ever conceived. It came to an end through the advance of technology as much under the sea as on the surface, which she had dominated. Her crown was to pass, much later, to the submarine; first, however, it went to the aircraft-carrier.

Chapter Three
CARRIER

*Without carriers we feel that we would have to revert to a
Coastguard type of Navy.*

ADMIRAL JAMES HOLLOWAY,
UNITED STATES NAVY,
Chief of Naval Operations, 1974–8

On 7 December 1941 naval aviation formally came of age. On
that Sunday morning an entire battle-fleet was eliminated by
naval air power. In just thirty minutes seven of the eight
battleships berthed in the United States naval base of Pearl
Harbor, Hawaii, were sunk or disabled by torpedoes and bombs
dropped by carrier-borne aircraft launched from Japanese
aircraft-carriers nearly 300 miles away. By this surprise attack
the United States was thrust into war, and she ceased, at the
same moment, to be the strongest naval power in the Pacific
Ocean.

Three days later, in the South China Sea, the British
battleship *Prince of Wales* and the battle-cruiser *Repulse* were
both quickly overwhelmed by torpedoes from shore-based
aircraft of the Japanese navy, flying from airfields 400 miles
distant. The two elements of Japanese naval aviation had
demonstrated their new and awesome power.

The aeroplane came quickly to naval warfare. In 1911, when all
aviation was primitive, an aircraft was landed on the deck of the
US Navy cruiser *Pennsylvania*. The next year saw a machine
flown from a launching platform on the Royal Navy battleship
Africa, anchored off Sheerness; the same pilot then flew from the
battleship *Hibernia*, under way off Portland. An elderly cruiser,
Hermes, became the world's first aircraft-carrier: she carried
three seaplanes (float planes), which were hoisted out to be flown

off the water, landed on the sea and then hoisted back on board.

In those early days the aeroplane (whether on floats or on wheels) and the lighter-than-air-ship were thought of only as scouting machines. The pilot and his observer could look beyond the horizon of the cruiser squadron that was traditionally employed to scout for the fleet: they could climb above the sea-level mists and the fog of battle that masked the view of the gunnery officer and his captain.

The aeroplane of 1914 could not fly very fast or very far; nor could it carry munitions in sufficient quantity to make it a useful weapons platform. To work with the fleet, it would have to be carried in a ship adapted for the purpose. The aeroplane had no runway and needed floats in order to take off from and land on the sea, so calm weather would be required. Its parent ship would have to stop to hoist out her machines and to recover them, which meant that she would have to drop out of the fleet formation and catch up afterwards. An ordinary aeroplane, without floats, could be flown off some improvised launching platform but would have to land ashore, and seaplanes could be launched on wheels that were then dropped in the sea, but with either method the parent ship would have to steam into the wind to help the pilot reach his flying speed. A ship of the line could not leave her station, and although a turntable launching platform—which was trained into the wind—went some way towards solving the problem, the aircraft still had to be recovered at the end of its flight. Battleships steaming fast and executing complex manoeuvres in close company could not conveniently stop; if they did, they were at greater risk from torpedo attack.

It quickly became clear that this clumsy and laborious procedure was not operationally acceptable and, moreover, that the performance of a float-plane could never match that of a land-based machine. Nor could reliance be placed, in those early days, on air support from ashore, for with the fleet well out to sea, land-based aircraft had neither the speed to reach the ships in time to take part in the battle nor the endurance to stay with the fleet long enough to be of much use. (This is still a problem for high-performance aircraft in the 1980s.) Somehow the admiral had to take his airfield to sea. A miniature floating airfield that could move with the fleet and could steam fast into wind to compensate for a very short runway, an airfield with a hangar to house the aircraft and workshops to maintain them—

these were the requirements for the newest type of warship, the aircraft-carrier. They still are today, and the basic means to satisfy those requirements are much the same.

By chance, a warship both large enough and fast enough already existed: the battle-cruiser. Of the five new battle-cruisers that joined the Grand Fleet after Jutland, three— *Courageous*, *Glorious*, and *Furious*—were to become aircraft-carriers. *Courageous* and *Glorious* proved failures as 'large light cruisers' (mounting 15-inch guns) and were rebuilt as carriers in the 1920s, but *Furious*, which was to have mounted two enormous 18-inch guns, the world's heaviest naval ordnance, was completed with only one. With a flight deck instead of her forward gun, she entered service as a hybrid battle-cruiser/aircraft-carrier. Aircraft could be flown off her but could not be landed, although Squadron Commander Dunning, of the Royal Naval Air Service, did once manage to swing his machine around the upperworks of the ship to land safely on the forward deck as *Furious* steamed into wind; in a second attempt, however, the aircraft careered over the side, and the brave Dunning was drowned.

Soon after this tragedy *Furious* was fitted with an after flight deck in place of the remaining 18-inch gun, but she kept her superstructure as a barrier between the two flight decks and remained unsafe for landings until she was stripped and rebuilt as a true carrier along with her half-sisters, *Courageous* and *Glorious*. All three served in the Second World War, but only *Furious* survived.

Meanwhile a converted passenger liner, HMS *Argus*, became the world's first true aircraft-carrier. *Argus* had a completely flush deck, and even her navigation bridge was retractable; but since any surface warship design must provide for bridge, mast and, usually, a funnel or at least a vent for the main engine exhaust fumes, the eventual solution was to incorporate bridge, mast and funnel in a superstructure displaced from the centre line to the starboard side of the flight deck. The 'island' design, as it has been called ever since, earned its inventor, a naval officer, an award of £500 from a grateful Admiralty.

With a clear flight deck now providing a 'runway' 40 or 50 yards wide and 200 yards long, although tiny by airfield standards, and rolling and pitching in any sort of sea, the carrier could launch her aircraft in tolerable safety, creating the additional lift needed by steaming fast into wind. Recovery too, though more difficult and hazardous, became a reasonable proposition for highly skilled pilots. A fence (known as the palisades) was raised and lowered at the forward end of the flight deck when aircraft were landing to safeguard other machines parked right forward and to prevent a pilot from overshooting into the sea. There was nothing as yet to prevent an aircraft that landed off the centre line from crashing into the island on the starboard side or diving into the sea (with very small chance of recovery) on the other. These hazards were greatly reduced, first, by arrester wires stretched across the deck, which engaged a hook underneath the aircraft, and, many years later, by a mirror landing sight, which ensured correct line-up on what had by then become an angled 'runway'. Ship-borne flying was difficult and dangerous in the early days, and it still is. While the technical problems were to be solved over the years, those of the organization, tactics and strategy of carrier operations were to prove much more difficult to solve, not least for historical reasons.

When the aeroplane had joined the Royal Navy, just before the First World War, it was as part of the battle-fleet, to which all other branches of the Service were subordinate. Most types of warship were deemed to be there simply to support the battle line of dreadnoughts. Squadrons of light cruisers scouted ahead of the fleet; battle-cruisers were intended to break up the enemy cruiser formations in order to prevent him from obtaining knowledge of the fleet's movements; destroyer flotillas screened the battleships from attack by torpedo-boats and submarines and themselves made torpedo attacks on the enemy battleships. Later, fleet submarines were to act as flotillas of submersible torpedo-boats. To this large, well-balanced and highly manoeuvrable force would be added the aeroplane. As more powerful machines appeared, the aeroplane would be more than a scout; it would become a flying weapons platform.

In the First World War, the British, German and American navies had airships as well as aeroplanes. The British sensibly copied the successful German design, but the airship proved too slow and too vulnerable for military work—although the non-rigid US Navy 'blimp' survived into the Second World War, operating off the East Coast of the United States, safe from attack by hostile aircraft.

Aviation made a disappointingly insignificant contribution to the battle-fleet action. At Jutland the five German airships were recalled because of the mists and the low cloud base, which also obliged the one British seaplane to fly at an altitude from which its observer could not keep both German and British ships in sight at the same time. His initial report was accurate but did not reach the commander of the scouting forces, who was anyway getting much the same information from his traditional source, the light cruisers. Mechanical failure cut short this solitary reconnaissance, and worsening weather prevented further seaplane flights.

Admirals accustomed to deploying heavy ships in line of battle saw no other immediate task for naval aviation until it became obvious that the numerically weaker German battle-fleet would not again challenge the Grand Fleet in surface action. Then officers like Beatty, who had succeeded Jellicoe as Commander-in-Chief, Grand Fleet, called for torpedo-carrying aircraft to attack the German and Austrian battle-fleets in harbour. However, suitable machines did not yet exist. In 1915 British seaplanes had made the first successful torpedo attack on ships at anchor; but against armoured warships larger, heavier torpedoes were required, and, to launch them, more powerful

7 The fleet carrier as she was in the Second World War: USS Oriksany (1945).

aircraft, which would not be seaplanes, for these could not take off with such a weapon load. The promised torpedo-carrying aircraft were slow in building, and the first such machines, embarked in the carrier *Argus*, arrived too late to be employed in the First World War.

The admirals had by now recognized another use for the aeroplane. With its cousins, the seaplane, the flying-boat and the airship, it was extensively employed on anti-submarine patrols and, most usefully, on convoy escort. The machines allocated to this work were often slow and of short endurance, and their only weapon was a bomb too small to damage the pressure-hull of a U-boat; but the mere presence of an aircraft was usually enough to make the U-boat captain dive, thus missing his chance to get into position, undetected, for a torpedo attack on the convoy. In the First World War aircraft did not sink U-boats, but they deterred them.

Ingrained mental attitudes of senior officers, compounded by the elementary state of the art, did not encourage progress, but an even greater obstacle now emerged. The Royal Flying Corps, which operated a central training establishment, had from the beginning a military and a naval wing, soon to be known respectively as the Royal Flying Corps and the Royal Naval Air Service. At first, the navy had been made responsible for the air defence of Britain because the army had taken most of its tiny air force to the Western Front. Against the sporadic—and militarily valueless—bombing attacks by German airships on English towns, the Royal Naval Air Service was ill-equipped and not very successful. The army took over air defence but fared no better. Bomber aircraft attacked London in daylight, causing damage of no military or economic importance but some loss of life. The understandable public outcry at the failure of the defence was one reason for the setting up of a War Cabinet Committee of Inquiry into the organization of aerial warfare. General Smuts was the chairman and driving force of the Committee, which recommended the creation of a new Service out of the Royal Naval Air Service and the Royal Flying Corps. It was thought desirable to centralize the procurement of aircraft, but underlying the recommendation was the belief that bombing might win wars. With no more evidence to support the case for strategic bombing than the apparent failure of the armies on the Western Front and the disappointing performance of the Royal Navy at Jutland, the Committee envisaged a future in which war would best be waged by bombing the enemy homeland in order to destroy his industry and communications, lay waste to his cities, kill and disable his civilians and thus frighten him into surrender.

Strategic bombing would be a considerable step beyond the ancient weapon of naval blockade. A blockade could throttle the enemy's trade and starve his industry. It could starve his civilians too, but this took a long time to accomplish. A strategic bomber force would leap over the enemy's army and fleet to achieve these objectives much more quickly and more economically. Henceforth, it was held, armies and navies were outdated, redundant. Such was the thinking of the new Service, and it was not surprising that, having gained the monopoly of aviation, the air marshals would stoutly resist any significant transfer of their newly won resources back to the army or navy in support of land or sea operations, which they regarded as irrelevant.

The Royal Naval Air Service had pioneered the aircraft-carrier; it had made the first successful aerial torpedo attack on shipping; it had led the way in 'strategic' bombing; for two years it had been responsible for Britain's defence against air attack. By the end of the war, however, it had become too large for purely maritime work. It was largely autonomous; few of its officers had any other naval experience, either at sea or through basic naval training; and most of them seemed to welcome the establishment of a third Service specializing in aviation, a Service, moreover, in which they could expect understanding and a more rewarding career. On 1 April 1918 the Royal Naval Air Service ceased to exist, and its 2500 aircraft and 55,000 personnel were absorbed into the new Royal Air Force, together with the army's Royal Flying Corps.

That the navy would continue to need aircraft in support and even afloat was not denied; but the long and heated argument about how to deploy them was decided in favour of the new Service, and so for the next twenty years the Royal Navy would uneasily share control of its ship-borne aviation with the RAF. An RAF contingent would go to sea, it was decided; it was even seriously proposed at first that since aircraft-carriers were in effect no more than floating mobile airfields, they should be under RAF command! The Admiralty fought off this challenge and retained operational control of the carriers, which were paid for out of the Navy Vote, as were the embarked aircraft; aircraft procurement was placed squarely in the hands of the Air

Ministry, however. The Admiralty could indicate only the desired characteristics of the machines it wanted, and, not surprisingly, these aircraft were not always of the best.

Naval officers specializing in aviation—though not observers—were attached to the RAF: a naval officer-pilot in the Fleet Air Arm (as it came to be known) also held a commission in the RAF. The Fleet Air Arm squadrons were thus a part of the RAF, and a naval aviator was unlike any other specialist who served in the various branches of the navy, such as submarines, or as a torpedo, gunnery, signals or navigation officer. In these early days a naval aviator could not expect to command a fleet or even a carrier. The resulting administration of naval aviation was a complicated nightmare; the skilled mechanics of various trades in the carriers belonged to the RAF, and the balance were naval ratings, though, when embarked, they were all subject to the Naval Discipline Act under the captain. On shore, in RAF establishments where training and operations were the responsibility of the new Service, all came under RAF discipline.

One more consequence of the creation of the third Service was that for a long time the Royal Navy lost its shore-based air squadrons. In the First World War the Royal Naval Air Service had been largely land-based and had employed much of its strength on anti-submarine patrols and convoy escort, with useful results. This branch of naval aviation was then designated Coastal Area and was perhaps regarded as the least important element of the RAF. When the Second World War began Coastal Command, as it had by then become, had few maritime aircraft suitable even for reconnaissance, much less attack. Its anti-submarine bomb was ineffective. For the protection of merchant shipping against air attack in home waters the Royal Navy had to look to RAF Fighter Command, but the problems associated with the control of interceptor aircraft at sea, beyond the reach of the elaborate home air-defence system, had yet to be mastered. For mine-laying, for strikes against enemy shipping, for attacks on warships, RAF Bomber Command had to provide most of the aircraft, but the RAF had paid scant attention to the torpedo, putting its faith in the free-falling bomb instead. In 1939 Coastal Command had only sixteen torpedo bombers, while Bomber Command airmen were not properly trained in ship recognition—a demanding task for any maritime aviator—nor in the technique of long-range navigation over the open sea that was needed if they were to find and attack their targets.

Since the air marshals showed such slight interest in maritime aviation, it is the more surprising that the admirals had, on the whole, failed to recognize the potential of the aircraft-carrier. It is even more remarkable that they had continued to build carriers, and in good measure, since in the early 1930s the Royal Navy actually outnumbered both the American and Japanese navies in this new type of ship.

The Fleet Air Arm—but not the shore-based Coastal Command of the RAF—was restored to the Royal Navy just before the Second World War. Only one of the Royal Navy's carriers, *Ark Royal*, was new, but six big fleet carriers were building, and all were to serve with distinction in the war. A force of 200-odd aircraft would grow sixfold by the war's end, but more than half would be American. Compared with contemporary American and Japanese machines, British naval aircraft were markedly inferior.

British naval aviation also lacked a well thought out and convincing doctrine. Its tasks remained as they had been designated nearly twenty years before—reconnaissance, defence against enemy aircraft and submarines and attacks on the enemy's heavy ships (but still only to slow him down to enable the battle-fleet to bring him to action). In the ensuing battle the Fleet Air Arm would spot for the big guns, because in the Royal Navy the aircraft-carrier was still regarded merely as an auxiliary to the battle-fleet. To most admirals the aircraft was a telescope, not a gun. Jutland still cast a long shadow.

This lack of doctrine and the failure to appreciate the potential of the new weapon, coupled with the geographical circumstances of the early days of the war, led to the mistaken employment of our large fleet carriers in the Western Approaches to the British Isles on U-boat hunting patrols. *Ark Royal* narrowly escaped being torpedoed, but *Courageous* was sunk, with heavy loss of life. The Norwegian campaign of 1940 demonstrated that a fleet could not be deployed within range of shore-based bombers and without adequate defence against air attack, for which high-performance interceptor-fighters were of more use than the anti-aircraft guns of the fleet. There were too few carriers, and they were unable to provide air defence either for the fleet or for the army units that were landed in Norway. As might have been expected after so many years of neglect, it proved difficult to co-ordinate naval operations with those of the RAF, and it took a long time to learn the lesson.

In the Mediterranean British sea power was always vulnerable to shore-based air power, first Italian and then, even more, German. Indeed, it was not until British and American air power was installed along the coasts of North Africa that the Allies could move freely in these waters. In the fighting for Crete and in the efforts to sustain the island fortress of Malta by large-scale naval operations in support of convoys, the Royal Navy suffered heavy losses. Ideally, its ships ought not to have been hazarded in these regions, and the carriers might have been better employed; but the Royal Navy could not choose where to fight, and it paid dearly for the legacy of history.

The picture is not all dark. The first major warship ever to be sunk by air attack, the cruiser *Königsberg*, was dive-bombed and sunk during the German invasion of Norway in 1940 by Fleet Air Arm squadrons based in the Orkneys. In the following year British naval aviation performed its auxiliary duty in exemplary fashion by undertaking torpedo attacks on *Bismarck* and disabling the German battleship with a lucky hit that jammed her rudders, so that she slowed down, steering erratically. She was then brought to action and sunk by a British battle squadron in the textbook manner.

Most carrier-borne torpedo-bombers had a crew of three and were slow. The British Swordfish (affectionately known as the 'stringbag') had a top speed of 139 miles per hour; the American Devastator, 206 miles per hour; the Japanese Kate, 235 miles per hour. By 1940 the state of the art permitted the air-launching of a torpedo weighing 1400 pounds (the standard ship's torpedo was more than twice as heavy), with an explosive warhead of 100 pounds, in such a way that it did not break up when it entered the sea and would run straight. The pilot had to maintain a steady speed and height until the release point; he would then be well inside the range of the enemy's guns, and in the open sea his target would usually manoeuvre to avoid the torpedo. To attack a fleet in harbour the airmen had to fly even lower and more slowly than usual, to ensure that their torpedoes did not strike the bottom after launching and that they settled quickly to their set running depth.

Between its successes against the *Königsberg* and *Bismarck* the Fleet Air Arm had achieved a victory of even greater significance, when a score of torpedo-bombers flew from the carrier *Illustrious* to attack the Italian naval base of Taranto at night. They sank three battleships at their moorings, and in so doing they at last fulfilled the wish of naval commanders a quarter of a century earlier who had been frustrated then by the lack of means. This British success at Taranto was carefully noted by the Japanese; they were to repeat the technique at Pearl Harbor on a vastly greater scale and with devastating effect.

High-level bombing of warships at sea was often less effective than the torpedo attack. The intended target manoeuvred to dodge free-fall bombs released from a great height. A 'stick' of bombs falling across a ship might merely straddle the target, and an armour-piercing bomb did no harm if it missed the ship by only a foot. Low-level bombing gave better results, especially when the pilot dived almost vertically on to his target. To fly so close to the warship's guns demanded great courage, but dive-bombers were very difficult targets for the anti-aircraft guns of the time and had a terrifying effect on the stoutest-hearted defence. In the Pacific campaigns the Japanese and American carrier-borne dive-bombers were particularly effective—especially against enemy carriers. Against armoured decks the release point had to be high enough for an armour-piercing bomb to attain sufficient velocity, but a well co-ordinated onslaught by high-level bombers, torpedo-bombers and dive-bombers with a strong fighter escort would overwhelm most defences.

The Royal Navy's Fleet Air Arm fought with skill and courage, but it was handicapped by its lack of high-performance aircraft and by a high command which, in the early days, had little understanding of maritime aviation. Both its eventual ally and its enemy were better placed. In the United States and Japan there was then no third Service, and both navies had retained full control of their maritime aviation, both ship-borne and shore-based, from the beginning. In these two navies an aviator could be confident that he was not in a professional backwater and was likely to get command of a carrier; there was no drain of aviation enthusiasts to a rival Service. That said, there was in the American and Japanese navies, as well as in the British, a strong and influential 'big-gun club'; America had seventeen battle-ships before Pearl Harbor, Japan nine and a battle-cruiser. In its own war games the US Navy ('Blue') was expected to fight an encounter battle like Jutland with the Japanese fleet ('Orange'). American carriers were to seek out and destroy the enemy carriers, but thereafter American naval aviation would spot for the guns of the battle-fleet. (It was still not thought that carrier-borne aircraft could destroy enemy battleships.) Although three years earlier Vice-Admiral King, in the carrier *Saratoga*, had successfully 'attacked' Pearl Harbor in the annual Fleet exercises, it is ironic that the American naval aviators' case was made so forcefully by the Japanese. The real onslaught, in December 1941, was on a dramatically larger scale.

The principal target of the 350 Japanese carrier-borne aircraft was the battle force, the eight dreadnoughts of the American Pacific Fleet, of which all but one were moored in 'Battleship Row'; the eighth, *Pennsylvania*, was in dry dock. The early morning of Sunday, 7 December 1941, seemed peaceful enough. The United States was not at war; many of the ships' officers and petty officers were on shore leave. In the fleet only a quarter of the anti-aircraft machine guns were manned, and their ammunition was stowed in locked boxes. At five minutes to eight, as on board each ship the colour party was preparing to hoist the Stars and Stripes, the first wave of Kates arrived over Pearl Harbor, launching their shallow-water torpedoes from heights as low as 40 feet, much as the Fleet Air Arm had done a year earlier at Taranto. Then the Vals dived down upon the ships dropping heavy bombs, one of which penetrated to *Arizona*'s magazines. She quickly became a blazing wreck, a tomb for 1100 of her company. Within half an hour three more dreadnoughts were to be lost and three crippled; only *Pennsylvania* escaped major damage. The Japanese aircraft had torn the heart out of the American battle-fleet. They had also struck a heavy blow at American air power, destroying scores of military aircraft parked neatly on airfields nearby. In two hours, their mission accomplished, most of the attackers returned safely to their ships. The Japanese naval air arm had achieved its aim of immobilizing the United States battleships, to prevent them from interfering with the astounding naval assault on British, American and Dutch possessions in the Pacific and South-East Asia. By happy chance, the American carriers were absent from Pearl Harbor that day, and that was, in the end, to prove fatal for Japan.

The two Pacific navies were about evenly matched in carriers when the war began—six Japanese to seven American. Several hundred Japanese carrier-borne aircraft, fighters and torpedo- and dive-bombers were augmented by some 500 seaplanes and flying-boats; of greater importance was the large fleet of shore-based twin-engined bombers that could carry a bigger torpedo further and faster. The shore-based naval aviators had always belonged completely to the navy and, as a result, were well trained in the technique of first finding and then attacking ships with torpedoes as well as bombs. The force that struck the British battleship *Prince of Wales* and her consort the battle-cruiser *Repulse* did not have to be hastily transferred from strategic bombing. These squadrons had been created, equipped and deployed precisely for that kind of warfare. Three days after Pearl Harbor was attacked they searched the South China Sea for their quarry and sank both great ships in ninety minutes. Out of eighty-five aircraft attacking—fifty-one of them torpedo-bombers—only three were lost to anti-aircraft fire, and there were no defending fighters. The lessons were quickly learned, and five months later, in the Coral Sea, another Japanese attack on a similar scale was a failure; the British Rear-Admiral Crace ordered his three big ships, two Australian cruisers and one American, to manoeuvre independently. All survived unharmed, although an accompanying destroyer was later very nearly hit by American land-based army bombers!

If trained specialist aviators could not always succeed against a resourceful enemy, the task was well-nigh impossible for hastily prepared squadrons, ill-trained and ill-equipped for the particular task. Just two months after the sinking of *Prince of Wales* and *Repulse* by naval aircraft flying from shore bases 400 miles away, the Germans provided a convincing demonstration of the unwisdom of twenty years of dual control of British maritime air power. The great battle-cruisers *Scharnhorst* and *Gneisenau* sailed boldly through the Straits of Dover, in full view and not 20 miles from the English coast, in daylight. Although the move had been foreseen, the Germans achieved a tactical surprise. The RAF disposed of some 800 aircraft in the south of England, but more than half of these were short-range fighters. Some 240 were day bombers, but only thirty-three were twin-engined torpedo-bombers, brought south in readiness, while the Royal Navy had stationed just six Swordfish torpedo aircraft on an RAF field in Kent. Routine air searches had failed to detect that the battle-cruisers and the heavy cruiser *Prinz Eugen* had left their base at Brest and were heading up the Channel, and when they were eventually sighted, the first formation to attack was 825 Squadron of the Fleet Air Arm, commanded by Lieutenant-Commander Eugene Esmonde. Every man perished in a most gallant but suicidal action, and Esmonde was posthumously awarded the Victoria Cross. No hits were obtained on the enemy; nor did the Coastal Command crews do any damage when they in turn attacked. Of 242 machines from Bomber Command, only thirty-nine managed to attack, and their general-purpose bombs would not pierce armour. The only success was obtained by mines, air-laid either in the preceding two weeks or—less likely—on the day itself; both *Scharnhorst* and *Gneisenau* were damaged, *Scharnhorst* seriously.

It was indeed a happy chance that no American aircraft-carriers were at Pearl Harbor when the battle-fleet was destroyed, for not only did the carriers escape attack, but they became the new battle-fleet. A heavy naval gun threw a 1-ton shell 20 miles at most; a carrier-borne aircraft could lift and launch almost that weight out to 300 miles and more. The aviator could see his target at close quarters; the gunnery officer of a battleship might see only tiny splashes, and perhaps flashes, in the distant murk and haze. This advantage was quickly appreciated by the Americans, who saw that in the aircraft they now had very long-range artillery. Once they had perfected the means of delivering torpedoes and bombs to a target in the open sea that was steaming fast, altering course rapidly, defended by gunfire and fighters, then the carrier could justly claim to have ousted the battleship and to have become the capital ship of the navy.

A land-based air force is deployed over many widely separated airfields situated well inside friendly territory. Furthermore, not only are the aircraft dispersed among several bases but they are also widely dispersed on each field. A carrier is obviously more vulnerable with all the elements of her small air force under one roof—the aircraft, their fuel, their ammunition, their bombs and torpedoes. Their 'friendly territory' extends no further than the radar picket destroyer a few miles away, and even the waters between are not always safe. Enemy submarines may penetrate the asdic (or sonar) screen. Of the five British carriers lost in the war, three were U-boat victims; of eleven American carriers lost, three were also sunk by submarine torpedoes. Even so, the carrier was no more and no less vulnerable to submarine attack than any other vessel, but she was the vital target for enemy airmen and submarines alike. The light fleet carrier USS *Princeton* was destroyed by just one bomb, which penetrated deep into the ship's interior. Unlike American carriers, the newer British fleet carriers were armoured on flight deck and sides to enable them to resist bombs and the 6-inch shells of cruisers. The British design, developed shortly before the Second World War, incorporated an armoured 'box' to protect the aircraft beneath the flight deck, though the price to be paid for this protection was that the ships could carry far fewer aircraft. In the war in the Mediterranean and in the *kamikaze* suicide attacks of the final year of the Pacific War this feature enabled the British ships to stand up well to punishment, while some American carriers were severely disabled by similar Japanese attacks.

For just two and a half years, from the Coral Sea in 1942 to Leyte Gulf in 1944, the line of battle was now formed by the carrier strike force, carriers fighting their own kind, as battleships had done for centuries. Cruisers and destroyers and even the fast battleships were in attendance to give extra fire-power against air attack, while destroyers screened the carriers from submarine attack. Another innovation for this new-look battle-fleet was its ability to remain at sea for several weeks, replenished under way by the fleet train—oilers, supply ships of every kind, repair ships and smaller aircraft-carriers with replacement aircraft. In the great sea fights of the Coral Sea and Midway in the months following Pearl Harbor, carrier fleet fought carrier fleet, though neither admiral ever saw his enemy's ships. In these and many other battles the American Commander-in-Chief profited by knowledge of his enemy's plans, an advantage which Jellicoe had not possessed at Jutland. Admiral Spruance combined shrewd judgement with reliable intelligence promptly relayed to him, and good fortune enabled him to catch the Japanese carriers at Midway in their most vulnerable state, with their aircraft on deck, refuelling and rearming. It was the American dive-bombers and not the gallantly flown torpedo-bombers that were decisive at Midway. Even so, the victory was hard won. Nearly 100 American carrier aircraft and the carrier *Yorktown* were lost; but American dive-bomber aircraft sank all four Japanese fleet carriers, destroying also 250 enemy aircraft. All of Japan's ten battleships (and a battle-cruiser) put to sea for this Battle of Midway, but none played any significant part. The three American carriers were not supported by a single battleship, even though an American battle-fleet of seven ships was available in the eastern Pacific. Fought just six months after Pearl Harbor, the Battle of Midway represents the high-water mark of the Japanese naval advance in the Pacific. Admiral Yamamoto had sought not only to attack and seize the island fortress and air base of Midway but also to bring the American Pacific Fleet—now inferior in numbers—to action in the old-fashioned way. He was disappointed, and although his battle-fleet remained in being, his carrier strike force did not. After this, its first defeat, the Japanese navy never recovered from the loss of so many trained carrier pilots; and by the end of 1944 Japan had ceased to employ her aviation in any but a desperate, suicidal manner.

These deliberate, organized suicide attacks began in late 1944 and were called *kamikaze*, which means 'divine wind' and is said to refer to the typhoon that scattered a Chinese invasion armada in the year 1570. The tactic was adopted because after their defeat at Midway few Japanese pilots could penetrate the screen of American fighter planes to hit their targets with bombs or torpedoes. It was easier for the Japanese to build the aircraft and persuade a fanatical hero simply to fly straight onto the nearest enemy carrier than it was to train pilots properly. Against this form of attack the light anti-aircraft automatic cannon— 20mm and 40mm—were seldom effective, being rather deterrents to a normal pilot; and even when such cannon shell did hit a *kamikaze* aircraft, it was usually too small to stop the craft or to deflect it from its course. For this it was necessary to hit with a far heavier projectile, as from the 5-inch gun. As *kamikaze* pilots often joined groups of friendly aircraft returning from a strike, they sometimes sneaked through undetected; but this ruse was countered by making friendly aircraft execute a full turn around a designated destroyer of the radar picket screen 60 miles out, while the Combat Air Patrol sorted sheep from goats. In the early days, a *kamikaze* pilot had a slightly better chance than one in four of hitting an American ship, and though this rate declined as defences improved, the far greater numbers of missions flown made the *kamikaze* a formidable weapon to the end.

Naval aviation was not confined to the large fleet carrier. Of the US Navy's 100 carriers at the war's end, only twenty were big ones, and most of the others were escort carriers—quick to build or convert from oil tankers, not very fast but able to carry up to thirty aircraft. Cheap enough to be risked on convoy escort and to provide air defence and anti-submarine patrol, they gave cover for amphibious operations and long-range bombardment in support of the army. The Royal Navy, which early on, in peacetime, had foreseen the need for smaller carriers for trade protection, took the same road and added more than forty escort carriers to the fleet. These had to play the carrier's part in the Battle of the Atlantic and the Russian convoys, and it was they and the newly created, very long-range, shore-based maritime air squadrons that helped to turn imminent defeat into ultimate victory. As the number of carriers grew, the battleships and the cruisers lost their spotter aircraft (which they had never liked anyway), while a new kind of ship-borne aircraft was brought into play with the advent of the interceptor-fighter catapulted from a merchant vessel in convoy. Especially effective against enemy reconnaissance aircraft shadowing the convoy well beyond gun range, it was a truly one-shot weapon; at the end of his mission, the pilot would have to land in the sea, close enough to a friendly ship to be picked up. This required a special sort of courage and skill; happily, most of the pilots were recovered safely and were able to fight again.

8 Escort carrier. A converted merchant ship, usually a tanker, was part of the team that defeated the U-boats in the Atlantic and on the Russian convoys. Escort carriers also gave air cover to amphibious operations in the Mediterranean and the Pacific. HMS Biter was one of forty escort carriers in the Royal Navy.

The Second World War thoroughly tested the theories of maritime aviation that some forward thinkers had developed in the 1920s and 1930s. It was as fierce and as demanding a conflict as any could have foreseen. War, as always, was a hard school in which to learn a new trade, but those who survived learned quickly. One lesson was that no naval commander could hope to survive long without air cover while his fleet was within range of enemy air power. Another lesson was that in mid-ocean, in those days at least, land-based aircraft could only be patrol types, with long endurance but low speed and only elementary weapons.

High-performance aircraft lacked the range to accompany a 'blue-water' fleet and, however fast they were, might still arrive too late to take part in the battle. To a considerable extent, this remains true today.

From both these lessons it quickly became clear that every naval commander, afloat or on shore, needed complete control of his air power. Aviation must be as much an integral part of his force—indeed, of his Service—as any surface vessel or submarine. All war experience had shown that shore-based interceptor aircraft dispatched to the defence of a convoy or fleet under air attack were effective only when a complicated system of fighter direction had been developed and practised thoroughly both ashore and in the ships. Far from land, where all the short-range aircraft would be ship-borne, such a system would naturally work better. Co-ordination with a separate Service in action has always been difficult.

Perhaps because the US Navy had always had control of its own shore-based, long-range maritime aviation, there was friction between that Service and the US Army Air Corps, which assigned some of its bomber formations to the maritime war. The US Army's long-range bombers flew anti-submarine patrols, and, in the Pacific especially, its aircraft were extensively employed in bombing attacks on enemy warships and shipping. The enthusiasm of the Army Air Corps sometimes outran its performance; its crews claimed—quite without justification—to have won the Battle of Midway, but they found ship recognition no easier than did the navy's aviators, and from the great height at which they normally dropped their bombs it was understandable that they might mistake a near miss for a hit.

It is ironic that the Japanese, with perhaps the best organization of maritime aviation, lost the war—though their defeat was not the consequence of any lack of professional prowess; it was, rather, the inevitable result of going to war with a nation that was much more powerful industrially, a nation that could outbuild their fleet and their air force many times over.

After the Pacific War was over an obvious question mark hung over the fast fleet carriers that had won the victory. There were those who held that since the carrier now had no other carriers to fight, there was little justification for such large and expensive warships, particularly when land-based aircraft could fly so much faster and further with a heavier load than before. The carrier, they said, should go the way of the battleship. Her defenders reacted sharply. The carrier had enabled the navy to win control of the sea, and now the same qualities enabled the navy to give instant local air defence where a land-based air force could not quickly establish airfields—and her fighter aircraft were now equal in performance to any land-based machines. She could launch attacks on enemy troops or ships with a variety of high-explosive bombs and missiles; she could protect herself with anti-submarine aircraft; her aircraft could lay mines in enemy waters. The carrier now promised to be more versatile than the battleship had ever been—and many times more powerful. And so the die was cast, and naval aviation remains the heart of the US Navy, with the big carriers of the generation built in the 1950s providing much of the tonnage of bombs dropped on Vietnam. They have formed the backbone of the United States Sixth Fleet in the Mediterranean for thirty years.

The 1950s had opened a Golden Age of the carrier, in the Royal Navy as in the US Navy. New devices appeared. The angled flight deck permitted maximum use of the whole deck and lessened the risk of collision with parked aircraft. The steam catapult reduced the take-off run required for the heavy jet-engined aircraft now entering service and used an abundant propellant—steam from the ship's boilers. The mirror landing sight enormously enhanced the safety of landing. Very advanced jet aircraft appeared, specially equipped for operation from the deck. The ship's radar and communications made a great leap forward. Greatly improved air-to-air, air-to-surface and anti-submarine guided missiles were embarked. With the modern carrier the most powerful conventional weapons system the world has ever seen had arrived.

Certain limitations remain. To launch and recover his aircraft the captain is still obliged to turn his ship into the wind, which is not always in the desired direction of advance. High-speed manoeuvring of the carrier and her attendant vessels causes high fuel consumption. One answer—for those who can afford it—lies in nuclear propulsion. *Nimitz*, 92,000 tons of steel and stores named in honour of one of the US Navy's greatest admirals, is a highly mobile military air base afloat, a home for more than 6000 men. She carries more than ninety aircraft—interceptor-fighters, strike aircraft, anti-submarine aircraft and some others carrying early-warning radar, electronic counter-measures equipment and the like. Nearly 1100 feet long, with a flight deck 240 feet wide, this great ship is powered by two nuclear reactors, which can drive her at 30 knots for thirteen years—nearly a million miles—without refuelling. Her combat aircraft are the equals of any land-based machines. Her aviators are trained to attack ships, or ground targets, or other aircraft with every weapon in the modern inventory. *Nimitz* is one of a dozen multi-purpose giant aircraft-carriers in the US Navy (though not all are nuclear-powered) whose ultimate mission is to be launching platforms for the attack aircraft that can carry nuclear weapons.

9 The US Navy has a dozen huge carriers, four of them nuclear-powered, as is USS Dwight D. Eisenhower, 90,000 tons, ninety aircraft. A carrier battle group includes cruiser, destroyers and frigates.

To replace the ageing British fleet carriers in the middle 1960s (at £200 million each) proved beyond the means of Britain, for the Royal Navy would have needed three large carriers to deploy an effective force. It did not get them. Instead the RAF was charged with providing the air cover that the fleet obviously needed, with high-performance, land-based aircraft. The fleet carrier then sailed out of the Royal Navy, and her remaining powerful fixed-wing aircraft flew to shore bases, some to fly with the RAF. For a time British ship-borne aviation had to consist of helicopters only, and even quite small ships were built or converted to embark and operate them.

British naval planners at once recommended the building of smaller carriers, but as it had been decreed that no more aircraft-carriers were to be built, the new type was at first described as a 'through-deck' or 'command' cruiser. In order to ensure that her anti-submarine helicopters could be operated to best advantage, her design incorporated a flat top and an 'island' superstructure, and this was to come in very handy when the small, vertical/short-take-off fixed-wing aircraft was adapted for sea service.

The Invincible-class ships are 'small', at 19,000 tons as against the 60–80,000 tons of the fleet carier and the 90,000-ton nuclear-powered ships. Each can accommodate only fourteen aircraft, mostly large anti-submarine helicopters, and five or six fighter/attack Sea Harriers. The 'Harrier Carrier' design incorporates the newest improvement to naval aviation, a ramp (sometimes called the 'ski-jump'), which allows the aircraft to take off with a much heavier payload. But the vertical/short-take-off aircraft is never likely to be in the same class as the very fast, powerful machines of the true fleet carrier, and it cannot be expected to succeed against high-performance, land-based

10 A Harrier aircraft takes off from the 'ski jump' of a 'Harrier Carrier', or anti-submarine cruiser. There are two other ships in this class, which is similar to the Soviet Kiev class and the projected US Navy sea-control ships.

strike aircraft. The 'Harrier Carrier' was designed not as a multi-purpose aircraft-carrier but as a platform for anti-submarine warfare. Her helicopters are her main armament, and her short-take-off fighters provide no more than local defence against surface ships and shadowers. She is not very different in this respect from the rather larger Russian Kiev class, described as 'large anti-submarine cruisers', a designation that allows them to transit the Dardanelles without breaching the Montreux Convention; while in American naval terms the Invincible class are 'sea-control ships', not aircraft-carriers. Nevertheless, they do give a task force commander at least that minimum of local air power which he will always need, together with excellent command and control facilities; though just three such vessels, with their escorts, must be deemed a very modest anti-submarine force for the North Atlantic and the Norwegian Sea. Many more small escort carriers were required in those regions in the Second World War to fight the convoy defensive battles against a much less daunting threat than that of today.

The US Navy was also beginning to find new fleet carriers expensive, though, as with other types of ship and weapons system, that moment came some twenty years later than it did in Britain. The case for the nuclear-powered carrier especially is not generally accepted within the US Navy, and the cost of a carrier battle group in which every ship is nuclear-powered is by now out of reach even of the Americans. Critics of nuclear power for surface ships argue that the equivalent of £1000 million that needs to be spent on a Nimitz-class carrier and the £600 million for the accompanying cruiser would be better spent on a larger number of smaller and cheaper oil-fuelled vessels; further, they point out that the other ships of the force, the destroyers and frigates that also accompany the carrier, are unlikely to be nuclear-powered (because of the even greater relative cost of putting a nuclear plant in a small hull), and if these have to be refuelled at sea, the main point of nuclear power for the big ships is largely lost.

It is argued too that the very large carrier is vulnerable to enemy submarines and missiles. They are, according to the contrary view, exceptionally well armed to protect themselves, and the US Navy remains adamant, as Admiral James Holloway, former Chief of Naval Operations, has made very clear. The large carrier, nuclear-powered or conventional, thus remains the capital ship of the US Navy. A dozen great ships like the conventional *Forrestal* or the nuclear-powered *Nimitz* will sail the oceans under the American flag until the end of the century and beyond. Older ships, such as *Forrestal*, completed in 1955, are being refurbished for the equivalent of a mere £250 million to fit them for a further twenty years or more of service.

By then the aircraft-carrier, as a distinct type of warship, will have lasted eighty years or more, a good deal longer than the steel-clad, steam-driven pre-*Dreadnought* battleship, and twice as long as the *Dreadnought* super-battleship which effectively spanned two world wars. Few of the individual pre-*Dreadnought* ships lasted as long as ten years; *Dreadnought* herself lived twelve years. Some of the 'super-dreadnoughts'—USS *Texas*, HMS *Warspite* and a few more—had their lives extended because of the Washington Naval Treaty. With modernization they lasted more than thirty years, but carriers like *Nimitz* and *Forrestal* will have had a useful life of half a century. Their endurance is a tribute to the excellence of naval architecture and construction and far exceeds that of any other modern weapons system, even much less complicated ones. It may therefore be said that if the carrier has taken the place of the dreadnought in power, she has more in common with the wooden-wall, line-of-battle sailing ship in longevity.

Chapter Four

GUNBOAT

The question of the small vessel for police duties will long be with us. Vice-Consuls and Resident Commissioners will, no doubt, continue to act on the great principle: when in doubt wire for a gunboat.

ADMIRAL OF THE FLEET LORD FISHER, 1905

In May 1961 the dictator of the Dominican Republic, Rafael Trujillo, who had been installed by the United States Government thirty-seven years earlier, was assassinated. In Washington there were fears of a Castro/Communist take-over or a return to the old illiberal regime, and to prevent this, the United States Government warned that it would not 'remain idle' if the Trujillos tried to restore the family dictatorship. Three days later the aircraft-carrier *Franklin D. Roosevelt*, a helicopter-carrier, a cruiser and twelve destroyers, with 1800 marines in amphibious vessels, appeared just outside the 3-mile limit, in full view of Santo Domingo, while jet fighters flew low along the coastline to underline the message. Next day the Trujillist plotters fled the country, and the threatened revolt did not take place. Gunboat diplomacy—first employed against the Dominicans in 1905—had, for the time being, ensured some form of democracy.

The gunboat was at first just that: a small vessel, powered by oars or sail, which could bring a heavy cannon across shallow waters in suport of naval or land forces. The gunboat was employed in the Baltic and in other parts of the world where 'blue-water' navies could not safely venture close inshore. Sailing ships of the line were out of their element in river estuaries. They needed room to manoeuvre, and they had to be kept clear of shoal water; besides, they made good targets for coast-defence guns.

Of the nineteenth-century triple revolution of steam, iron and modern artillery, steam reached the gunboat before the battleship. In the 1820s the kingdom of Burma was ripped open by three little steam gunboats, which penetrated 500 miles up the Irrawaddy and all along the coasts in support of a venture by the East India Company. These gunboats were floating artillery batteries; more than that, they were river tugs that hauled sailing vessels against wind and current, and they were even troop transports. In the 1830s gunboats—not only those of the Royal Navy—steamed up the Niger, the Euphrates and the Nile and opened up the Pearl River and the Yangtse. Gunboats were busy in Burma again and then in Tonkin and Annam, where France was beginning her conquest of Indo-China. In the space of sixty years much of Africa and of South and East Asia had been penetrated and conquered, or colonies had been planted and trading posts established, largely by the use of the steam gunboat. Especially in wild, trackless regions, the waterways were the highways of the explorer, the trader, the missionary, the soldier. The progress of the steam gunboat was hindered only by human frailty; until tropical fever could be brought under control the European was seriously inhibited in his advance through Africa. Together, steam and quinine made it possible.

At first the 'blue-water' sailors were rightly cautious. The steam engine was in its infancy and not yet reliable. Its clumsy paddles could be smashed by enemy shot, and they worked efficiently only in calm water, which effectively restricted such vessels to rivers and protected waterways; besides, paddle wheels were large and took up valuable space that might otherwise be used for guns or soldiers. Moreover, the paddle steamer was slow and therefore quite unsuitable for a fleet action; she was thus well out of the mainstream of contemporary naval doctrine.

The wooden hull proved too weak to bear the load of steam engines and heavy artillery in a shallow-draught vessel. For the steam-powered screw something else was needed, an iron hull. Iron was strong and flexible in ways that timbers could not be. Once built with an iron hull, with steadily improving engine design and a screw instead of paddle wheels, the steam gunboat became strong, safe and fast. She could be large enough to accommodate engines and artillery, yet of light enough draught to operate in shallow water, and in an iron rather than a wooden hull, her stokehold was less of a hazard. The steam gunboat had the supreme advantage for her purpose: she was independent of wind and current.

Steam required coal, and the early steam engines used a lot of it, so the penetration of the interior was dependent on strategically located stocks of coal, and the coaling stations of the European merchant colonists soon appeared around the world. The steam gunboat was employed in the Crimean War and in the second Opium War (1856–60) to haul sailing ships of the line into positions from which their broadside could bear on the enemy forts. It was then that the revolution was complete. At Sebastopol the Allied navies learned to their cost how vulnerable the wooden three-decker was to modern artillery placed in a fortress. The ironclad followed quickly, and the long duel between armour-plate and armour-piercing shell began.

Not all the gunboats were iron-hulled or of shallow draught. The Royal Navy's gunboat flotilla that was employed—with slight success—against the Russians in the Crimea and the Baltic comprised some vessels that were wooden-hulled and of deeper draught than 'river gunboats', designed for offensive operations off an enemy coast. The concept reached its peak in the coast-defence ship, which enjoyed brief favour from the late 1850s, when British public opinion began to be influenced by the renewed danger of war with France. With the coming of the marine steam engine, coastal raids became a bogey, as did the threat of close blockade of the coast and of British ports, perhaps attack on the great naval bases of Portsmouth, Devonport and Chatham—and even invasion.

Recent experience of naval operations against Russia and in the American Civil War had indicated that such coastal warfare might come again, and that if it did, armour, heavy artillery and shallow draught would be of value. There emerged a slow, unhandy, unseaworthy but heavily armed and armoured type of warship. These coast-defence ships and the heavy coastal gunboats were no more than floating versions of the many new forts which were built close inshore to defend the principal naval dockyards. They did not last long and were soon abandoned in favour of the orthodox battleship, which could do the coast-defence job and fight a fleet action too.

The threat of such small, heavily armed, inshore bombardment vessels did, however, mean that the safety of the realm and the security of the home base could no longer be guaranteed by the Admiralty alone, especially now that the raiding cruiser, or the invasion transport, was no longer dependent on the wind. Indeed, the invasion scare was to recur many times, even when the Royal Navy possessed overwhelming strength in almost every type of warship, especially in battleships and cruisers (as, for example, in 1914, when one-third of the British Expeditionary Force was kept at home in case of a German invasion). The recurring invasion scare lasted a century all told. The numerous heavy coastal artillery batteries hastily installed after Dunkirk were not finally dismantled until 1956.

Against the warships or the armies of another European power the gunboat could not prevail, and she was not expected to. For such encounters the cruiser was the appropriate warship. But the gunboat was highly effective when employed to obtain concessions from weaker, non-European nations and from tribal rulers whose military strength was insignificant. For such small colonial wars or for subsequent policing use was made sometimes of the sloop, a general-purpose patrol vessel for work offshore as well as in river estuaries, and sometimes of the river gunboat, which, though smaller, was often more heavily armed. Neither type was designed to fight her own kind, unlike battleships or cruisers. Usually, when two colonial powers (the term here embraces the United States as well as the Europeans) collided, one would transfer its interest a few miles along the coast or up-river to avoid actual conflict. Indeed, the gunboat, by preserving existing gains, often acted in support of a mutual colonial cause, for national 'zones of influence' were usually respected by the empire-builders in the face of a common threat.

The Golden Age of the gunboat lasted throughout the era of British maritime supremacy, from the end of the Napoleonic (or French) wars to the 1880s, and for a considerable time thereafter in localized spheres of influence, such as on the China Station. The Boxer Rising led to a remarkably successful example of an improvised international 'police operation', involving the troops of several European powers and their warships. In the later years of this *Pax Britannica* sloops were still employed in North American waters, on fishery protection duties and in 'showing the flag'. In the Solomon Islands, as late as 1903, a British gunboat, HMS *Sparrow*, was to shell a village as reprisal for the murder of a missionary. A pair of steel gunboats patrolled the West African rivers for Britain right into the 1920s. However, the heyday of the gunboat—except for China—belongs to the nineteenth century.

In the first sixty years of the *Pax Britannica* the absence of any other powerful navy apart from the French made it possible for Britain to police the maritime world by gunboat and by cruiser at remarkably little expense. Of course, the gunboats were supported by the fleet in being, the line-of-battle ships, far distant, without whose invisible backing the flimsy naval presence could not have been long sustained. A naval captain knew that he represented that unseen armada, that vast arsenal of naval power, the mere existence of which enabled him to exercise authority on behalf of the local British consul or magistrate that was out of all proportion to the actual force at his command.

For much of this long period gunboats were to be employed chiefly in the protection of trade—all trade, not merely British trade. Throughout the nineteenth century France too maintained a large navy and also extended her imperial power and influence across Africa, large parts of Asia and the Pacific. There was occasional friction where the edges of the rival empires touched, but the French annexation of huge territories in North and West Africa, throughout Indo-China and across the southwest Pacific was not seriously challenged by Britain. French trading posts and concessions were also established along the great ocean highways; French warships sailed along the coasts of Africa, Asia and Latin America; and French gunboats steamed up the Yangtse River, along with those of the Queen. The gunboat was the warship for the age of free trade, before the age of imperial rivalry began in the final quarter of the nineteenth century.

The gunboat was cheap, so she was the ideal instrument for protecting distant national interests and for punishing injury to Europeans or disrespect to their flags. The concept is neatly expressed by Professor Laurence Martin:

> A wide variety of naval activities is conducted in peacetime for the express purpose of bringing home to others the power, and particularly the naval power, of the country in question.
>
> The conception that ships are small mobile pieces of national sovereignty makes them particularly suitable to symbolize the nation from which they come. For the same reason governments have always paid punctilious attention to the manner in which their vessels and flag are treated, and to the reception they accord other nations.
>
> *The Sea in Modern Strategy*, 1971

Although, beyond the reach of her artillery and her landing parties with rifles and, in later years, the Maxim machine-gun, the gunboat might have rather less effect than was commonly imagined, yet it was this sort of man-of-war and the small cruisers that wrote one of the finest chapters in the history of the Royal Navy. After the slave trade was formally abandoned by Britain in 1807, the Royal Navy was henceforth employed in putting down the traffic between West Africa and the Americas and between East Africa and Arabia. The West African slave trade was already large by then and growing yet larger, amounting to a traffic of some 80,000 to 130,000 slaves a year throughout the first half of the nineteenth century. Anti-slavery patrol was the navy's most dreary task, uncongenial and dangerous, a duty performed in the worst of climates, but performed faithfully for fifty years, despite the great hardships endured by the ships' companies (in one year alone more than a quarter of the men of the West Africa squadron died of fever). The Admiralty grumbled at the expense, yet there was no suggestion from officers or men that anti-slavery patrols should be given up. Other Governments were, in the main, either unhelpful or openly hostile, though by the middle of the nineteenth century most civilized states had concluded treaties with Britain outlawing the slave trade and requiring ships' masters to co-operate with the officers of the patrolling gunboats and other ships. However, to stop and search a suspected slaving vessel was seldom made easy. The United States in particular, although she had forbidden the import of slaves as early as 1808, for long denied Britain the right of search on the high seas; and not until 1861, four years before the Congress abolished the institution of slavery, did President Lincoln permit the examination of ships flying the American flag.

Dealing with a slaving vessel was also a complex business, even when she had been stopped and detained. The British captain had as his first duty the care of the liberated slaves; he was required to land them safely in a place where they would not be enslaved again. He then had to sail his prize to the nearest British port, where the slaver's captain and crew would be put on trial. If a conviction were obtained, the British man-of-war's captain and crew were entitled to a share of the proceeds of the sale of the slaver, but they seldom got anything.

No less arduous was the same service off the coast of East Africa, although slavery was never completely eradicated in this region. But the part played by the Royal Navy in the (albeit partial) suppression of this loathsome traffic is a shining example of the proper use of limited force in support of moral attitudes and in strict accordance with international law. Not for the first time, idealism prospered under the guns of a warship. The record of the anti-slavery patrol stands up well, especially against the uglier side of the Opium Wars.

There were other tasks for the gunboat. Pirates swarmed everywhere outside European and North American waters. The corsairs of the Barbary Coast had their base bombarded by the Royal Navy, though the nuisance was ended only by the French annexation of Algiers. In the South Seas, the Caribbean, the East Indies, the Persian Gulf and on the China coast, the Royal Navy was to hunt pirates for a hundred years. In the early years of the twentieth century a cruiser in the Gulf would detach a sub-lieutenant and half a dozen seamen, armed with rifles, for patrol in the ship's whaler. The coasts were unlit and not well charted; sometimes a boat and its occupants vanished without trace.

The captain of a gunboat or of any other of Her Majesty's men-of-war in the nineteenth century was expected to be

11 The Pax Britannica. *The gunboat HMS* Vulture *at Mozambique in 1873.*

familiar with international law. 'Instructions for the Guidance of Commanding Officers' were supplied, giving the text of every treaty concluded with every other nation, as well as technical notes for the measurement of prizes. Any naval officer could see, for example, that on 18 March 1852 a Commander Strange, of Her Majesty's ship *Archer*, had signed a treaty with the 'Chiefs of Badagry'—an important trading centre in what is now Nigeria—in the unhealthy Bight of Benin ('where one comes out for forty goes in') on the Slave Coast. Not only did the Chiefs of Badagry renounce slavery, but they also promised 'complete protection . . . to missionaries or ministers of the Gospel'.

If the gunboats were the world's maritime policemen, alas, there were never enough of them to put down slavery, to end piracy, to protect missionaries and 'extend the benefits of civilization'. As one First Lord of the Admiralty consoled himself, 'It is fortunate the world is not larger, for there is no other limit to the service of the fleets.'

However, from the 1880s the pace of technological change had quickened, as we have already noted. Large and powerful warships were under construction; in Britain the recurring invasion scare led to increases in the Estimates, the building of yet larger vessels and the scrapping of smaller, older craft. Not the gunboat but the battleship, the armoured cruiser and the torpedo-boat destroyer were to be the important vessels of the Royal Navy. The *Pax Britannica*, upheld for so long by the gunboat and the small cruiser, was ending, while most of the great European powers had joined the race to annex the remaining regions of Africa and Asia. In *Heart of Darkness*, published in 1902, Joseph Conrad described the scramble for empire thus:

> Once, I remember, we came upon a man-of-war anchored off the coast. There wasn't even a shed there, and she was shelling the bush. It appears the French had one of their wars going on thereabouts. Her ensign drooped limp like a rag; the muzzles of the long 6-inch guns stuck out all over the low hull; the greasy, slimy, swell swung her up lazily and let her down, swaying her thin masts. In the empty immensity of earth, sky, and water, there she was, incomprehensible, firing into a continent.

The old-style 'gunboat'—river gunboat, sloop, small cruiser— was no more than a cheap, mobile, floating platform for a naval officer, with just enough armament for him to be taken seriously.

The new imperialism required larger military expeditions and more powerful warships, as the great powers advanced across Africa and South-East Asia, now confronting each other. For this new venture the Royal Navy comprised what Jackie Fisher, the First Sea Lord, described as too many ships 'too weak to fight, too slow to run away'. He bravely formulated and drove through a policy of rationalization, scrapping 150 gunboats and cruisers in order to concentrate men and material on the modern big-gun fleet that he was convinced he must build up in home waters. By now France had been replaced by Germany as Britain's rival at sea, and the newly building German battle-fleet gave cause for alarm both in the British Admiralty and among the public. Now, it seemed, the fate of the British Empire would be decided not in the oceans across the globe but in the North Sea. Every seaman in a gunboat in Asian or African waters was one fewer for the modern dreadnoughts on which Fisher believed that command of the sea rested.

Excepting the coast-defence ship, which enjoyed brief popularity, the gunboat, as police vessel, was not expected to stand up to a modern warship, but she was a manifestation of British sea power in distant waters. Furthermore, she had been a most reliable instrument of colonial and foreign policy—so much so that the Foreign Office, arguing for more rather than fewer naval police vessels, noted there were 'important British interests in distant seas where the opportune presence of a British ship of war may avert a disaster which can only be remedied later at much inconvenience and considerable sacrifice'. Not only were 'important British interests' at stake; there would also be numerous occasions for the Royal Navy to come to the aid of some hard-pressed community hit by storms, earthquake or other natural disaster. Thus Fisher's ruthless scrapping policy was not welcomed by the old-style diplomat. Yet it was not merely the technical requirements of the modern battle-fleet but also the change in the nature of the task that had altered the Royal Navy's posture in much of the world from that of policeman to that of watchful, heavily armoured warrior.

Not all the gunboats were scrapped. On the China Station they were to have their busiest years in the twentieth century, and the flotillas there were then at their most numerous. In the 1920s more than forty river gunboats—British, American, French, Japanese and Italian—patrolled the Yangtse. The British and French navies had employed gunboats to survey the channels of the great Chinese rivers from the 1860s onwards. A few colonial annexations (Hong Kong, Macao, Kiaochow, Weihaiwei), the Treaty Ports (Shanghai, Ningpo, Foochow, Amoy, Canton), the concessions, where foreigners had their own courts of law and their own police, and numerous consulates and factories and mission stations—all these required protection. The great rivers which facilitated trade made this sort of policing easy.

The classic British river gunboat was of the Insect class, built in the First World War to a scheme of Admiral Fisher, who proposed to send a flotilla up the Danube to fight the Austro-Hungarian river gunboat flotilla. Only one Insect reached the Danube, and only after hostilities had ended, but some steamed up the River Dvina in Latvia during the war of intervention following the Russian Revolution; most went to China. This useful class were sizeable craft of 600 tons with a speed of 14 knots, and they mounted two 6-inch guns and various lighter weapons, especially machine-guns, while other classes mounted a howitzer, necessary for shooting over high ground. On the Yangtse, river gunboats like these made a reasonably comfortable home for two officers, half a dozen petty officers and leading hands out of a ship's complement of twenty-five, augmented by Chinese cooks and stewards.

In the 1920s and 1930s China was in turmoil. River warlords fought each other; in 1927 the Kuomintang broke with the Chinese Communists; five years later the Japanese attacked China. The gunboats were always busy. Naval officers had a large measure of discretion, and some commanding officers were more robust in their dealings with the Chinese authorities than the law might strictly have allowed. As reprisal for a riot or the murder of a European, occasionally naval bombardment of a town was threatened unless the Chinese authorities could produce their own scapegoats—whom they usually shot without trial to satisfy the senior foreign naval officer present. Very occasionally, towns were actually bombarded by gunboats and even cruisers. By a people who held life cheap and were accustomed to rough and ready justice, such high-handed methods were quietly accepted, and commanding officers of the gunboat flotilla seldom went too far in their task of saving European lives and property. The British, who bore the main burden of this work, were, it could fairly be argued, only attempting to perform the duty of the barely visible Chinese authority, yet legends remained of excessive force used by the foreigners in their gunboats. 'Gunboat diplomacy' began to take on its pejorative modern meaning. By the early 1930s, as the Japanese invasion brought real war to the great rivers, the gunboats began to look out of place, and they were soon to be outnumbered by the cruisers and destroyers of the great powers.

12 The imperial policeman. HMS Gnat, a river gunboat of the Insect class.

When Japan attacked British and American possessions in the Pacific and the Far East in 1941, the flotillas on the China Station were quickly overwhelmed, and after the defeat of Japan at the end of the Pacific War there were to be no more gunboats in China, though other warships, chiefly sloops, destroyers, mine-sweepers and smaller craft, continued the tradition for a short time. Then the Kuomintang Government collapsed, yielding to the Communists. As the Communist armies swept across the Yangtse in the final stages of the civil war, it was the British frigate *Amethyst* that fought the very last classic gunboat action in China. Caught in the advance, she was heavily damaged by Communist army artillery and only extricated herself much later with great difficulty and courage. In the waters around Hong Kong Royal Navy ships still occasionally hunted pirates, and twenty years later British mine-sweepers and other small ships were to be active in the Straits of Malacca in the 'confrontation' between Malaysia and Indonesia.

In the two world wars the gunboat was employed in her other traditional role as inshore bombardment vessel, as in the 1914 expedition against the German colony in the Cameroons and in the much bigger campaign in Mesopotamia. During the Irish Easter Rising of 1916 there was even a gunboat in the River Liffey, bombarding the rebels in Dublin. Twenty-five years later some of the little gunboats brought away from the China Station to serve in the Mediterranean carried out shore bombardments in support of the army, just as other gunboats had done ninety years earlier in Crimean waters. The river gunboat's 6-inch guns were cruiser-size, but even heavier weapons were doing the same job afloat in the coastal monitor, a vessel of shallow draught, usually mounting a pair of battleship's guns. The monitor was employed by the Royal Navy in both world wars even in Western Europe. This strange warship was effectively a siege battery afloat. Her target was stationary, and so was she. Her gunnery officer could afford the time for the fairly leisurely business of finding the range and then lobbing heavy shells into the target area slowly and deliberately. Two big guns were sufficient, but the monitor could not provide rapid, concentrated fire in support of a landing (though she was sometimes wrongly employed in such operations), and she could only operate when naval (and later air) supremacy had been assured.

For concentrated 'drenching' fire on assault beaches con-verted landing craft, with their similar characteristics of shallow draught and inshore mobility, were employed in what might be called a gunboat role during the Second World War. Some mount-ed a 25-pounder army field gun, others multiple high-explosive rockets. Even stranger variants or combinations appeared, but none was to continue as a regular type of warship once this specialized job was done.

If, as Clausewitz held, war is 'a continuation of political commerce by other means', then navies are well suited to the task of exerting diplomatic pressure, using limited force and offering a wide range of threats. In peacetime every fighting ship may be employed as a 'gunboat', and even the largest warships have done duty as the instruments of gunboat diplomacy. During the Spanish Civil War the battleship *Royal Oak* interposed herself between a rebel cruiser and a Government refugee ship; and nearly forty years later the aircraft-carrier *Eagle* was dispatched to give physical (as well as moral) support to the Zambian Government, which feared air attack by the illegal regime in Southern Rhodesia.

Gunboat diplomacy has had many more important successes in the twentieth century. The American naval concentration in Cuban waters in 1933 certainly achieved its main purpose, which was to help to secure the installation of a pro-American Government; and when that Government was overthrown, more American warships, including a battleship, assisted through their presence in the formation of a 'reasonably conservative' Cuban Government. Nearly thirty years later, in April 1961, the visible presence of the US Navy in those same waters certainly encouraged those engaged in the foolish and ill-conceived 'Bay of Pigs' venture, which failed for many reasons, not the least of which was that actual American naval support was very sensibly withheld. A month later, as we have noted, a similar initiative was to prevent a revolution in the Dominican Republic, though the operation had to be repeated four years later. Clearly, for success modern gunboat diplomacy depends very much on a very clear perception by diplomatists of the nature, and hence the likely reactions, of the Government or country that is the target of a naval demonstration of force. What failed in Cuba could still succeed in the Dominican Republic. Diplomacy, not the gunboat, is to blame if the ploy goes wrong.

The earlier cheap, flexible instrument of gunboat diplomacy for use against primitive societies and weak forces cannot be used against military equals without incurring grave risks—unless the naval force is seen to be acting within its rights, within what is mutually understood to be its proper geopolitical sphere of influence. Thus the US Navy's 'selective blockade' of Cuba during the 1962 missile crisis was successful not only because of the limited (and obviously defensive) nature of the action, but also because the Soviet navy could not concentrate a comparable force in Cuban waters. The gunboat acting outside her Government's sphere of influence is now likely to be challenged or ignored. Gunboat diplomacy has historically been based on bluff, and today that bluff may well be called.

Both the Anglo-French expedition to Suez in 1956 and its 'harassment' by the US Sixth Fleet must be regarded as unsuccessful gunboat diplomacy—the former, because of the international response it aroused; the latter, because the Amer-

ican force commander obviously could not carry out his
'threats'. Nearly twenty years later that same Sixth Fleet did not
attempt to halt the Turkish sea-borne invasion of Cyprus.
Those who contemplate gunboat diplomacy today must weigh
very carefully the risks of upsetting the delicate balance of forces
in the region concerned, and they must also reckon with the
possibility of intervention, military or diplomatic, by the super-
powers or by supra-national bodies. The world has shrunk and is
consequently harder to police today than it was fifty years ago.

*13 Mobile
imperial police
station, the
second-class
cruiser HMS
Medusa (1888).*

Some tasks outside this awkward diplomatic area remain
constant, and for them every man-of-war may be considered a
gunboat. All warships have a duty to police the seas, to put down
slavery and piracy, to go to the aid of other mariners in distress
and to help foreign Governments and communities, when asked,
in the aftermath of natural disasters. All these tasks are well suited
to the warship, which has, for her own purposes, the necessary

resources of trained men and specialized equipment, including those for communications, fire-fighting, rescue and salvage (afloat or ashore) and repairs to ships and homes. The warship also has the means to feed the hungry, to tend the sick and injured, to restore electricity and water supplies, even to provide a body of armed, disciplined men to maintain order. Any warship can, and does, provide any or all of these services in international waters and in the territorial waters of others by invitation.

Strangely, it is in home waters and in time of peace that the role of the gunboat has become uncertain. In war there are obvious jobs for the descendants of the worldwide 'policeman' so far described, such as mine clearance, coastal convoy escort and the inshore defence of ports and harbours. In peace an enormously diverse range of tasks has to be done on, over and under the sea, but the clear lines of responsibility for them have become, almost inevitably, blurred between several Departments of State. One may think at once of the protection of offshore energy installations against terrorist or even clandestine enemy attacks; marine fire-fighting and salvage; search and rescue; traffic control in the Straits of Dover and other busy narrow channels; counter-measures against oil spillages or other potential hazards from tankers; prevention of the intrusion into territorial waters of potentially hostile ships, submarines and even aircraft; and above all, perhaps, the protection of fish (though not the fishermen, as they themselves suppose).

In home waters the Royal Navy is quite properly subordinate to the civil power in nearly all these matters. The Fishery Protection Squadron effectively operates under the administrative orders of the Ministry of Agriculture, Fisheries and Food (though Scotland has a separate Department). The Customs and Excise 'Waterguard' and the civil police can call on the Royal Navy for assistance. The Department of Trade, with responsibility for shipping and pollution, the Department of Energy, which is concerned with offshore gas and oil installations, the Home Office, in charge of frontier control and immigration, policing and the regulation of communications—all these and other Departments of State can and often do require the Royal Navy to provide transport across the sea, to give military support and to do what could reasonably be expected of civil authorities—or even of private individuals or firms, such as salvage companies. The Coastguard is the co-ordinating authority responsible for marine search and rescue both inshore and well out to sea and for traffic control in the Dover Straits. The division of labour is far from logical; for example, a naval officer shares with a civilian agency the duty of inspecting fishing boats and measuring their nets, but he is not required to enforce the Factories Act on an oil platform or the Merchant Shipping Act on the high seas. Around our long and irregular coastline pilotage lights are maintained by Trinity House and the Commissioners for Northern and Irish Lights, bodies on which the Admiralty is represented together with shipping interests. The Royal National Lifeboat Institution is a wholly voluntary agency; many lives are also saved at sea each year by the crews of Royal Navy and RAF helicopters. The responsibility of police forces and county fire brigades extends to the limit of territorial waters and beyond, but few police launches or fire tenders can venture safely even as far as the 12-mile limit, let alone to the edge of the 200-mile exclusive economic zone. Consequently, the Royal Navy or the RAF will sometimes have to convey police or any other agents of the civil power to an oil rig or a ship (wherever a customs or police launch cannot reach), though often civil helicopters or supply vessels serving the oil rigs may be the obvious means of transport.

The Royal Navy's part in the policing of Britain's sea frontier is a large one, comprising patrols by offshore craft as well as by mine counter-measures vessels and the much larger frigates and destroyers. Together with the RAF's maritime reconnaissance aircraft, these ships provide a police presence all around the coast. The standard offshore patrol vessel, or 'administrative escort vessel', is of trawler rather than warship design; she is relatively slow and not easy to manoeuvre, having only one screw, unlike most other warships. With fewer bulkheads and watertight compartments, she cannot sustain serious collision or under-water damage. Her single 40mm automatic gun is almost symbolic: more often than not, it is covered so as not to alarm other mariners. Although classed as a fighting ship of the Royal Navy, with the wartime task of defending Britain's offshore resources, especially oil-rig platforms, she is essentially a maritime police vessel, very much in the style of the old gunboat. In home waters she belongs to the Fishery Protection Squadron, whose task is to patrol the fishing grounds in British waters in order to safeguard stocks. The captain's navigation must be exact, since he will be required to produce his charts in evidence for the magistrates if he arrests and prosecutes a poacher. He must have extensive knowledge of the fisheries and other resources of his country's exclusive economic zone, and he must be familiar with constantly changing legislation. His communications with his Government are instant, and in cypher, secure from eavesdroppers. He must be cautious and polite in his dealings with foreign fishermen especially, since the diplomatic consequences of a mistake could be far-reaching. He takes his instructions not from the Ministry of Defence but from the Ministry of Agriculture, Food and Fisheries. The system works reasonably well, but it is not logical; nor is it easy to understand. Moreover, as offshore activity increases, the traditional British expedient of expecting the armed forces to undertake essentially civilian tasks simply because no one else is capable of doing so may not serve as well in the coming years as it has in the past.

Under the present system the chain of command and control is unwieldy and fragmented; too many different organizations, public and private, are involved. A second problem is that the wrong equipment often has to be used for lack of any other. In the Icelandic cod wars the Royal Navy learned to its cost that expensive and heavily armed but thin-skinned frigates were quite unsuited to gunboat duty against the small, sturdy Icelandic patrol boats. The fast frigate and the long-range maritime reconnaissance aircraft are both designed and intended to deter war or to fight it; but gunboat actions, especially on one's own doorstep, ought not to be practised by vessels clearly intended for war unless there is no argument about the rights and wrongs of the affair. The third, and perhaps the most serious, objection to present practice is that the military functions of the state should be separated from the police function, except, of course, in time of natural disaster. The armed forces are political instruments wielded by the Government of the day, whereas the police are (or ought to be) independent; and while they are, of course, loyal to the Crown, their business is enforcing the law and answering to the courts. The danger is not that officers of the Armed Services cannot be relied upon to behave in a constitutional manner, but that they could appear to be usurping the function of the policeman, the proper representative of the civil power.

A respectable solution has been found in some countries which maintain coastguard services that undertake all the duties mentioned above and, though armed, are seen to be quite separate from the military, at least in time of peace. In Britain such a service could thus amalgamate the functions of the existing Coastguard with those of the Fishery Protection Squadron, but it would also require its own 'air force', with more aircraft than at present, together with helicopters for search and rescue, and it would assume sole responsibility for the policing of the sea frontier. The Royal Navy and RAF would be freed from many 'civil' tasks and could better prepare to deter war, although their services would still be available in aid to the civil power, as they always have been. The parallel with the day before yesterday is obvious. Jackie Fisher scrapped 150 men of war that were 'too weak to fight, too slow to run away' in order to build his battle-fleet. What he overlooked was that those little warships were intended neither to fight nor to run away; they were maritime police vessels and as such, did not really belong to a modern navy, any more than do the offshore patrol vessels of today, the descendants of the gunboats of the *Pax Britannica*.

14 Today's gunboat stays at home: Royal Navy Fishery Protection Vessel, Leeds Castle.

Chapter Five

COMMANDO

He that commands the sea is at great liberty, and may take as much or as little of the Warre as he will.

FRANCIS BACON,
Of the True Greatness of Kingdoms and Estates, 1597

On 26 January 1945 a force of 500 Royal Marines disembarked from the larger ships of the East Indies Fleet to seize and hold the island of Cheduba, off the coast of Burma. After four days they were relieved by the army, whereupon the marines rejoined their ships, and that very afternoon they were manning the heavy guns of the cruisers bombarding coastal defences in support of the soldiers. The official history of the battle noted: 'The Commanding Officer of the marines remarked in his report that it was doubtful whether so rapid a switch from sea to land and back again to sea could be found even in the long story of his regiment's work on both elements.'

The commando connection is more than three centuries old. In the days of the line-of-battle sailing ship sailors and soldiers were interchangeable, as they had long been, and under Cromwell's Commonwealth all admirals were generals first, as was Blake. In the Anglo-Dutch wars Prince Rupert and General Monk employed their troops to man the fleet, the men returning to duty ashore when the ships were laid up in winter.

The Royal Marines properly date from 1664, with the raising of the Duke of York and Albany's Maritime Regiment of Foot, known also as the Lord High Admiral's Regiment. In 1685 the Admiral's Regiment became Prince George of Denmark's Regiment, but after the Revolution of 1688 it was disbanded, together with several other units thought to have been infiltrated by Catholics and therefore supposed to be loyal to the former king. Almost at once, however, the continued need for sea-soldiers was recognized by the raising of more regiments of marines for hostilities only, to be disbanded at the end of each war, until the eventual creation of a regular marine corps under Admiralty control as a permanent part of the Royal Navy. These marines were enlisted soldiers who had sworn an oath of allegiance to the Crown and so were generally considered more reliable than the seamen, most of whom were not volunteers but pressed men and none of whom had taken an oath of loyalty. Marines on board ship were permanently under arms, and they drilled as soldiers. In dress and bearing they were distinct from the less strictly disciplined sailors, living apart from the rest of the lower deck. The marine detachment, on parade or with sentries posted, was often the only reliable body of men on whom a captain might depend to uphold his authority.

In spite of this not always enviable reputation, the marines have sometimes shown no greater loyalty to authority than the seamen, for at Spithead and the Nore in 1797 marines joined the mutineers, as did some at Invergordon in 1931. Indeed, in the nineteenth century marines seem to have had just as high a serious crime rate as the sailors, though this may have been accounted for largely by their even more rigorous discipline. The onboard policing function of the marines (who only became 'Royal' as late as 1802) has long since diminished with the creation of a naval ship's police force to support the Master-at-Arms, and the formation of the Regulating, or Provost, Branch of the Service.

In their early days marines were the only trained infantry available to a naval commander, with the exception of army regiments occasionally embarked for sea service. (This is still the case today.) As such, they proved most useful in landing parties and boarding parties, providing musket fire and wielding bayonets. Afloat their fighting task was to act as sharpshooters high in the rigging, sniping at enemy officers who were easily recognizable as they stood on the quarterdeck, habitually in full dress uniform. (Nelson, for instance, was fatally wounded by a musket-ball fired by a French marine in the tops of the *Redoubtable* at a range of a few feet.) The marines were considered to be at the disposal of the naval High Command, and a marine officer could seldom expect to attain the highest ranks in the Corps, such posts being usually reserved for admirals as sinecures. When Nelson reached flag rank he also drew the pay of a colonel of marines, as was the custom, although he certainly had sufficient fighting experience alongside the Corps, both ashore and afloat, to make this seemly.

The eighteenth century and the 'Great War' with France (as it was then known) in the early years of the nineteenth century were the grand years for a maritime strategy employing amphibious forces principally in the Mediterranean and the Caribbean. In scores of engagements the Royal Navy and its marines boldly stormed and seized harbours, fortresses and islands. Many of these, in the long peace after Waterloo, would serve as coaling stations for the steam-driven fleets of the future. The marines also fought alongside army regiments in the Peninsular War and in North America, notably at Bunker Hill. A feature of some of these campaigns was the successful combined or 'conjoint' operation (as it was then termed) to land a sizeable army from the sea, as for the capture of New York in 1776—though there were failures too, as at Charleston.

The marines fought with the musket and bayonet, as we have seen, while the sailors who often accompanied them carried cutlasses and sometimes pistols, but neither marines nor sailors were to escape the coming technological revolution. As the effective range of heavy naval ordnance increased, the marines lost their battle function as sharpshooters. Their musket-ball would not carry as far as the new shells, and their target, the officer on deck, was now behind armour-plate. The marines were given a new fighting task afloat, that of sharing with the sailors the manning of the ship's big guns, while the marine bandsmen were later to take over the operation of much of the complex fire-control equipment. One of the after heavy-gun turrets of a modern British battleship, 'X' turret, became one of the traditional action stations of the marine detachment, together with two or more of the 6-inch or other secondary-armament guns. By tradition, and as a reminder of the unruly past, the 'barracks' were still to be found right aft on the lower deck, between the wardroom and the rest of the ship's company.

The romantic style of eighteenth-century naval campaigns that resulted in the steady capture of islands in the West Indies and the Indian Ocean gave way, after the defeat of Napoleon, to a more deliberate extension of the bounds of empire and of the worldwide area of British influence. The acquisition of territory was the prelude to policing, and by the end of the nineteenth century small colonial garrisons were scattered across the globe. A revolt or an invasion would have to be dealt with first by the local police and such native troops as were still loyal, often backed up by volunteers from the colonial settler population. The first reinforcements, if they were needed, would almost certainly be a party of sailors and marines landed from a man-of-war, a gunboat or cruiser detached from the squadron nearest to the scene. All seamen, and stokers too, received regular instruction on the rifle range, and the pistol and the cutlass were standard weapons. Machine-guns, mounted on board ship for use against torpedo-boats, were often landed with the detachment for the more serious incidents. The bluejackets made good use of their shipboard skills once they disembarked, with seamen gunners handling the 12-pounder field pieces that were carried for the purpose in all battleships and cruisers. The annual field gun display at the Royal Tournament represents very accurately the sort of shore role for which these guns were used and their crews trained. Like army sappers, torpedo-men were trained to use explosive demolition charges, and other ratings in the landing party were visual signallers, wireless telegraphists, cooks and medical orderlies. Seamen were adept at improvising bridging and lifting gear and were accustomed to handling small boats with awkward loads. This they had demonstrated in the most remarkable way when they hauled Wolfe's guns up 300 feet of nearly vertical cliff to the Heights of Abraham and thus made possible his capture of Quebec. Landing parties were popular work for sailors and marines alike, who looked forward to escaping from their confined quarters on board ship. There would be excitement, and the officers especially could expect promotion should one of their seniors be killed.

In some campaigns these landing parties were formed into a naval brigade that was intended to take its place in the line with regular army units, but because marines spent most of their service in small shipboard detachments, their officers gained little staff experience or understanding of the operational problems of larger formations. When a naval contingent was landed for action, the ship's gunnery officer would see to the ammunition; the paymaster would arrange for food; the first lieutenant organized the transport; the torpedo lieutenant would supervise demolitions; and communications were in naval hands. Command of the force was often withheld from the only professional soldier present, the 'major of marines' (whatever his actual rank), and given instead to a naval officer, probably the ship's executive officer or the gunnery officer.

In what has been aptly called 'the long afternoon' of Queen Victoria's reign, British imperial power was sustained by British sea power. In dozens of colonial rebellions and local wars, sailors and marines were frequently employed as colonial infantry. The idea was sound enough while warfare remained relatively uncomplicated both at sea and on shore, but from the 1880s onwards the increasing complexity of naval ordnance required highly skilled specialists, and although the marines were well enough trained to switch instantly from their duties on board ship to those ashore, their dual role was wasteful and weakened the ship's fighting capacity. If any substantial number of sailors had to be landed with them, the parent ship, whether cruiser or gunboat, would no longer be able to do her job at sea. This was a situation which captains and their admirals sought to avoid at all costs, certainly after the turn of the century.

Although sea service was their principal duty, the marines were always a useful force for emergencies ashore. If it was thought that a campaign might last several weeks or even longer, and if more men were required than could be provided by one cruiser, a Royal Marine battalion would be assembled from the marine detachments of all the ships in the Fleet, as was done during the Boxer Rising; though complete battalions raised at home for an expedition such as the Egyptian Campaign of 1882 were less common. The marines remained a small corps, firmly integrated with the navy's organization, though trained in the basic military skills on army lines and thus compatible with army units. In 1914, at the outbreak of Britain's first major European war for half a century, no senior naval officer had direct experience of fighting a modern naval battle (though there had been observers at Tsushima in the Russo-Japanese War), but almost every British admiral had seen action at some time in his career, in a naval brigade or landing party. One of them had won the Victoria Cross in ferocious hand-to-hand combat in the Sudanese Campaign, that fine seaman Arthur Wilson, who became First Sea Lord shortly before the First World War.

Wilson's background, the romantic age of Victorian empire-building, was to prove a disadvantage when he assumed the wider responsibilities of this great office and led him to misjudge the form and nature of a future major war, as well as to overestimate the value of such naval auxiliaries to a land campaign. Nor was he alone in this. For the previous ten years and more the War Office and the Admiralty had been making quite separate plans for quite different scenarios. The generals, naturally enough, favoured a 'continental' strategy, under which a British army would fight in France and Belgium, while the admirals wished to see their marines, and the army too, as mobile forces operating on the flanks of the likely enemy, Germany. Under the guns of the fleet, troops would be landed on the North German islands and coasts to neutralize or invest the German naval dockyards and to establish forward bases for the Royal Navy's light forces. Admiral Sir John Fisher, who had been recalled for a second tour as First Sea Lord on the outbreak of war, urged a descent on the German Baltic coast. Under his energetic direction large numbers of shallow-draught lighters were constructed, the forerunners of the landing-craft of a later day, but they were never employed in this imaginative scheme because the War Office had no troops to spare. Moreover, there were sound military objections to it, for even if the army had gained a lodgement, it would surely have been defeated by the much larger forces that would speedily have been brought up by the excellent German railway system. In the event—and, as it turned out, regrettably—the scene of amphibious operations was to be not the Baltic but the entrance to the Black Sea. To force the Dardanelles Straits, to knock Turkey out of the war, to open a supply route to the Russian armies, the Royal Navy alone was ordered to 'bombard and take the Gallipoli Peninsula, with Constantinople as the objective'. Before the real attempt had started a battle-cruiser had shelled the forts guarding the entrance to the narrows, but this had merely alerted the defenders. In the purely naval assault that followed, shore batteries were bombarded and marines and naval demolition parties were landed, but after repeated attempts and the loss of several large warships, it had to be conceded that the fleet could not 'take' the peninsula. In the Dardanelles Campaign proper which followed, a large Allied army made an opposed landing, but after eight months of fearful losses, it was recognized that the operation could not succeed, and the troops were brought off again by the Royal Navy. The only other somewhat similar venture of that war was the earlier brief attempt to save the Belgian fortress of Antwerp in 1914, when the newly formed Naval Division, which included a brigade of marines, operated independently of the British army fighting in Belgium and France. This too was unsuccessful, and after the Dardanelles episode, the Naval Division was kept in being to fight in the trenches, far from salt water; and although they did so with conspicuous skill and gallantry, it was at the expense of the role at sea for which they had enlisted and been trained. Thus it was only at the Dardanelles and later at Zeebrugge that the Royal Navy and the marines were able to practise the difficult art of amphibious warfare.

The neglect of the historically successful commando idea continued between the wars. As the official historian noted, 'In the Royal Marines we possessed a corps with a centuries-old tradition for amphibious warfare; yet in 1939 we were employing them almost exclusively to man a proportion of the armaments of our big ships.' There were certainly some marines organized to fight on shore, but these formed the elaborate 'mobile naval base defence organization', which included anti-aircraft defences and was an indication of the separate strategic views of army and navy. In 1939 the British Army was again committed to a 'continental' strategy, and, as in the previous war, considerable formations of troops operated as part of a much larger allied army, with the decisive battles fought some distance from the sea, in eastern Belgium and northern France. Amphibious warfare was never envisaged by those who saw no merit in storming bullet-swept beaches when one could safely disembark in a well equipped port. As long as Britain had a powerful field army on the mainland of Europe, sharing the front with other Allied armies, a British amphibious force had nowhere to go. The generals argued that there was little point in trying to open another front, and that the Royal Navy should be able to prevent the enemy from attempting it. Thus the British believed that a German invasion of Norway would be impossible in the face of the Royal Navy and the RAF. Ironically, the Norwegian General Staff had reasoned that only the British could invade Norway and that such a thing would not happen because Britain had no need of Norway. Unknown to the Norwegians, there was in 1940 a plan to land an Anglo-French force in northern Norway, to pass troops through Sweden to fight in Finland against the Soviet army; mercifully, as it turned out, the Finnish war ended before this could be put into effect, but a fresh plan was made to land troops in Norway if and when the Germans invaded that country in response to the defensive mining of Norwegian coastal waters to stop the traffic in iron ore destined for Germany. As it happened, eight British battalions and a French force were opposed by fifty-one German battalions, which quite soon carried out the seaborne invasion that it had been thought only the British could mount. In a country with such a long, indented coastline, it would have been natural to employ amphibious forces against the invaders, but the maritime contribution amounted to no more than a few hundred sailors and marines hastily landed from ships of the fleet, with no specialized equipment. In April 1940 the Royal Navy possessed just ten landing craft; five years later there would be 5000, with 150 landing ships for good measure.

This early defeat on the Northern Flank in Norway, and the rather surprising collapse and surrender of France, drove the entire British Army from the mainland of Europe; its evacuation through Dunkirk has passed into the folklore of gallantry and improvisation in defeat, though it is hardly part of the commando story. Britain now stood alone, and even the defence of the realm was in grave doubt; but it was already clear that if Germany were to be defeated, it would be on the continent, and that one day the Royal Navy would have to land a large army again in order to reopen the Western Front, quite certainly against fierce opposition. So the Royal Navy was forced to study amphibious warfare again, to learn again how to land troops on a heavily defended coastline and how to keep them supplied and reinforced across open beaches until ports could be captured and cleared. While the armies were being raised, equipped and trained, while the landing-craft were being built and the crews found for them, a period of many months, even years, would obviously be needed during which valuable experience could be gained and equipment tested in amphibious warfare on a very small scale along the 2000 miles of enemy coast that now stretched from North Cape to the Pyrenees. The commandos were back in business, but because of the deployment of the Royal Marines on board ship or in base defence units, none could be spared from these higher-priority tasks of the Corps, and the first specialist raiding parties (known as 'commandos' after the South African Boers forty years earlier) were army units; it was two years before the formation of the first Royal Marines Commando. The first commando raid took place on Midsummer's night 1940, a few hours before the Armistice took France out of the war. Just over a hundred raiders, in four groups, attempted to land on the French coast, with varying success. Commando raiding continued on a modest scale, and for the most part the raids achieved little of any military significance, though in the next two years the possession of sea power enabled more distant targets to be selected, in the Lofoten Islands off northern Norway and at St Nazaire. The commando idea was largely of psychological importance at this stage. Britain was too weak for more than the occasional small-scale foray, and the raiders could do little serious harm. Their greatest feat was at St Nazaire, where they put out of action the one dry dock on the west coast of France that could take the battleship *Tirpitz*. The raiding policy owed much to the hopes entertained by the British leadership that raids on the coast of Western Europe would be complementary to the resistance movements in the occupied countries and might well encourage a popular revolt that would drive out the German occupation troops and so make a long, hard-fought land campaign shorter or even unnecessary. However far-fetched these notions might seem with hindsight, commando raids were cheap, and they undoubtedly kept up the British people's spirits at a deeply depressing time. Britain had been thrust out of the land war, and, apart from the aerial bombing of Germany and the time-honoured maritime blockade, there was little other offensive action that could be taken in those grim years of isolation and desperation.

15 A weapon familiar to Nelson: a converted tank-landing craft fires a salvo of rockets at beach defences, 1944.

Any such commando raid, however, was dwarfed by the full-scale opposed landing, the invasion of the mainland of Europe. Not only scale but also the technical difficulties were of a quite different order. It is never easy to land troops on a defended beach. With no friendly harbour available, transports and supply ships would have to be unloaded in deep water, and the soldiers, with their equipment, ferried ashore in small craft. This was bound to be a lengthy and laborious process, and suicidal against well placed and well armed defences. Accordingly, specialized craft of all sizes had to be designed that could beach quickly and safely and float off again. For a sailor, trained always to keep his ship well clear of the shore, to run aground is to be grossly negligent. A new skill had to be acquired, and marines in large numbers were trained to handle small landing-craft. The marines claimed to be better suited to the business of deliberate grounding because while a sailor on the beach is out of his element, a marine is a sea-soldier, a true amphibian.

The most ambitious raid of all, that on Dieppe in northern France in August 1942, was really a sort of dress rehearsal for the eventual invasion of Europe, and as such it was quite different from the previous raids. Dieppe was attacked by two brigades of regular infantry—nearly 5000 Canadians, with a tank regiment as well; the commando units present were assigned the task of acting as shock troops, their aim the destruction of enemy batteries on the flanks. Dieppe was a costly failure; nearly 4000 of the 6000 troops were lost. Some valuable lessons had been learned, however, and the Normandy landings in June 1944 were planned in the light of that hard-won experience. Any attempt to capture a harbour—as at Dieppe—was abandoned; in the D-Day landings the troops assaulted across the beaches and brought their own harbours and breakwaters—the 'Mulberry' concept. The Normandy landings were made on five separate beaches by two American and three British and Canadian divisions, with largely British naval support. The defences were heavily bombarded, and the assault was made in daylight.

The invasion of Sicily and then of Italy, at Salerno and later Anzio, had also been 'regular' operations, in which complete army divisions were embarked, transported long distances and safely landed on the beaches, though the troops then had a fierce fight to advance inland. Commando troops were employed in these large-scale assaults, but again in their shock capacity. Their orders were to seize particular strong points or other important objectives, for which their specialized skills, such as cliff-scaling, would be useful. The Royal Marines were prominent in these battles, but they were to dominate some later actions, as at Walcheren, to secure the approaches to the great port of Antwerp. This is as good an example as any of the development of amphibious warfare. The marines provided the 'light infantry' for the assault and also crewed most of the landing craft; Walcheren showed how amphibious warfare might be conducted for a maritime objective, since Antwerp was to become the chief port supplying the Allied armies in the Low Countries. Marine commandos were, naturally enough, loaned to the army for tasks requiring their specialized skills, such as the crossing of the Rhine, but unlike in the First World War, there was no Naval Division, with its marine brigade, committed to a land front. In the Second World War the Royal Marines reached a peak strength of 80,000, ten times their present number.

Although not truly part of the commando story, being on a massively grander scale, the US Marine Corps has been closely modelled on the Royal Marines. American marines have their own history of imperial policing, from the early nineteenth century onwards, in North Africa, Central America, the Philippines and China. They too had contributed forces to the Western Front in the First World War; but after 1918 they did not neglect amphibious warfare, as Britain did. Between the two wars opposed landings were practised on a large scale, and the troops, the specialized landing-craft and amphibious tracked vehicles, and the techniques of assault, had been carefully prepared. The heavily armed US Marine battalions, regiments and even divisions that stormed ashore to capture one Japanese island fortress after another, from the Solomons to Okinawa, were not the product of brilliant but hasty improvisation, as were the British commando units, but regular formations with a well defined mission of capture and consolidation in the manner of a military offensive on land. This was an entirely different concept from that of the commando raid undertaken by a very small, almost irregular unit of lightly armed troops hoping to achieve surprise while carefully avoiding action with the enemy's main forces, which promptly withdrew when they had accomplished their strictly limited task. The US Marine Corps has continued to prepare for amphibious warfare on a massive scale, as befits its strength, which reached half a million in 1945 and is today, in peacetime, much bigger than the entire British Army! With their own engineer assault troops, armour and artillery, as well as their own infantry, the US marines also have their own combat aviation squadrons; and complete marine divisions fought in major land operations alongside the US Army in Korea and in Vietnam.

For a medium-sized power, activities on such a scale were out of the question, and Britain's marines happily developed in the strictly maritime direction. Although immediately after the Second World War the British Army retained a strong interest in amphibious warfare, the continual drain of 'colonial' policing, from the Middle East, through South-East Asia, Africa and Cyprus to Northern Ireland, has long since relegated the study of those techniques to the background. For important political reasons, for more than a generation the vast bulk of the British Army has been deployed on the North German plain with other Allied armies. The marines have thus become the natural source of small, highly specialized, commando units undertaking a variety of low-intensity missions, while detachments in ships, though now less important than they were, still account for a proportion of the Corps. The marines are traditionally jealous of their near self-sufficiency and insist on crewing their landing-craft and flying their own 'regimental' helicopters. The larger troop-carrying machines, however, are provided by the Royal Navy, which also finds their doctors, dentists, chaplains, schoolmasters and mechanical engineers to maintain their landing-craft. Nearly all the military skills—until recently, even truck-driving—are taught by marine rather than army in-structors.

Fortuitously, the virtual end of empire assisted in the evol-ution of the commando function. The gradual abandonment of fixed naval and military bases and garrisons round the world enhanced the importance of global sea power, for only the Royal Navy could fill the vacuum, and only to some extent. In the late 1950s the Golden Age of the Royal Marine commando forces began. They were complementary to the fleet of that time, and they implemented the strategy of a naval power with worldwide responsibilities. Royal Marine commando forces made the first-ever assault landing by helicopter, in 1956 at Suez. They fought with skill and daring in Borneo and Sarawak during the 'confrontation' with Indonesia. Marines suppressed army mutin-ies in the infant states of Uganda and Tanzania, though their enduring task was to share with the army the burden of 'counterinsurgency' campaigning (for which their amphibious skills were seldom needed) in Malaya, Cyprus, Aden and, of course, Northern Ireland. In their true role, neither a huge army nor a handful of raiders, but a brigade or regimental-size formation of light infantry was embarked, first in converted aircraft-carriers and then also in specialized 'assault' ships. Air power was provided by the fleet carriers around which the Royal Navy was grouped, a true 'blue-water' navy.

16 Landing craft in the battle for the approaches to Antwerp, 1944.

The Royal Marines have faced repeated threats to their existence as a Corps. Just after the last war their value was questioned, and then twenty years later, and it is being questioned again today. The Admiralty, which has twice lost its shore-based aviation to a third Service and now much of its ship-borne high-performance air arm, has consistently defended its marines. The first threat was easily countered by their Lord-ships' grave assertion that disbandment was impossible because the marines provided the Royal Navy's ceremonial music! More recently, a threat came from the army, which resented what it regarded as no more than infantry being under the control of another Service. A new crisis came for the marines when the last of the aircraft-carriers sailed into the breaker's yard, and when the Royal Navy was redeployed to the English Channel and the eastern Atlantic, a change reminiscent of Admiral Sir John Fisher's regrouping of British naval strength in the North Sea in the early years of the twentieth century.

The Royal Marines, however, survived their translation to home waters by adapting to a European strategy which is, of necessity, part-maritime. Three Commando Brigade was redeployed from Malaysia to the United Kingdom, and, together with a company of Dutch marines, now comprises the first Allied reinforcements to the Northern Flank of the North Atlantic Treaty Organization (NATO) in Norway and Denmark. Some 2000 strong, they are essentially highly specialized light infantry with their own tracked over-snow vehicles, anti-tank weapons and attached artillery. Sea power enables the parent ships, the assault ships and a commando-carrier to hold the troops in readiness for days, if need be, out of sight 'over the horizon', yet within a few hours' steaming from their intended point of disembarkation, which need not be a port. The marines thus enjoy strategic mobility and can reach a battlefield quickly and quietly. Once there, the tactical mobility conferred by helicopters, by small, fast landing-craft and by tracked vehicles provides a quite remarkable flexibility in rapid deployment. To the landsman the harsh mountainous coastline of northern Norway, deeply indented by fjords, is an almost impassable barrier to movement, but not for marines equipped and trained for the job. By contrast, air-transported forces lose much of their mobility on arrival in such terrain, even if airfields are still available. Such land forces cannot quickly or reliably bring with them their transport or heavy (and mobile) weapons, and even if these essentials are stock-piled in advance or provided by the host country, movement must still be restricted to the few roads in regions as desolate as this.

Three Commando Brigade, together with Dutch and American marines and Norwegian troops, are a powerful deterrent to a Soviet invasion of northern Norway, but the forestalling of that rather unlikely contingency is secondary to the truly maritime purpose of safeguarding the military installations for which northern Norway is important. The value of this remote territory lies in its geographical position athwart the 'choke point' of the only practicable exit from the Barents Sea. The Soviet Union's Northern Fleet, her largest, faces a harder task than did Hitler's navy, for to gain the Atlantic, Soviet ships, aircraft and submarines must pass northern Norway, and it is there that the chain of radar stations and underwater listening posts that extends from Greenland, Iceland and the Faroes is made complete. Deprived of that forward link in the chain of sensors, the NATO fleets would find it much harder to win a future battle of the Atlantic, since so much now depends on the peacetime tracking of surface vessels and submarines from the earliest possible moment. To win the battle of the Atlantic, it would first be necessary to win the battle of the Barents and Norwegian seas. In the front line of this battle would be the marines.

17 Tactical mobility. Royal Marines move easily about the battlefield.

The marines can thus still lay just claim to being an essential component of a maritime strategy, and they even make use of some of the same elements; for example, their commando-carrier, having disembarked her military 'passengers and cargo', departs for her other mission, that of fighting a purely naval

battle as an anti-submarine helicopter-carrier. It is not, however, the shape or size of the marine force itself that qualifies it
for inclusion in the story of sea power. A coastal raiding party
may as readily move 1000 yards or 1000 miles; an entire brigade
of troops may execute an outflanking manoeuvre by landing
further along the coast. Both activities require the skills of
amphibious warfare and the local air-lift afforded by sea-borne
helicopters, but, with some retraining, both could perhaps be
performed by conventional soldiers. What distinguishes the
marine commando concept is the mixture of tactical and
strategic mobility that is also the hallmark of a 'blue-water' fleet.

18 Strategic mobility. The assault ship brings troops, tanks and guns to the battlefield.

A coast-defence navy comprising short-range patrol vessels, even one stiffened by submarines and aircraft, cannot project sea power across oceans, and any marines it has will be merely the adjuncts of a 'continental' strategy, operating on the seaward flank of the army in the same fashion as Soviet naval infantry did until very recently. Indeed, the dramatic Soviet emergence in the world's oceans included the appearance of marine-assault landing ships, no longer confined to the Baltic and Black seas but now seen daily in the Indian Ocean, the Arabian Sea, off East and West Africa and as far afield as Vietnam. Thus employed, marine forces, whether British, American or Soviet, are genuine components of sea power. It is only a 'blue-water' navy that makes it possible thus to position ground forces reasonably close to a crisis point but also to keep them over the horizon, to furnish them with immediate heavy support in terms of both weapons and protection and to withdraw them quickly and without fuss. These are important attributes of sea power.

Chapter Six

CRUISER

Our great reliance is on the vigilance and activity of our cruisers.

ADMIRAL LORD ST VINCENT, 1803

At eight minutes past six on the morning of 13 December 1939, when the Second World War was barely three months old, three British cruisers were lying 150 miles off the mouth of the River Plate. Their commander, Commodore Harwood, reasoned that here he might find the German heavily armoured cruiser, or 'pocket battleship', *Graf Spee*, now at large in the South Atlantic and destroying commerce. Harwood detached one of his ships to investigate smoke sighted to the north-west, and very soon came the report, 'I think it is a pocket battleship.' It was. Early on, Harwood's most powerful unit, the 8-inch gun cruiser *Exeter*, was crippled by the enemy's 11-inch guns. Then *Ajax* was badly damaged, but it was *Graf Spee* that fled to the sanctuary of neutral Montevideo, where she was scuttled to avoid capture. In her brief sortie she had accounted for only nine merchantmen.

The battle-fleet guaranteed sea power: the cruisers put it into practice. In this sense a 'cruiser' could be almost any man-of-war *not* in the line of battle, but in modern times the term 'cruiser' has come to mean the largest fighting unit able to function without auxiliaries and the smallest vessel capable of nearly every form of naval activity, from scouting and policing to fighting—a complete navy, it might be said, in one hull.

The designation 'cruiser' indicates her principal task, which has always been long-range patrolling, and from this requirement flows her chief attribute of endurance. A cruiser must also be large enough to keep the sea in any weather; fast enough to be the 'eyes of the fleet', to scout and shadow, to overhaul the enemy in a chase; and powerful enough to overwhelm that enemy with her guns, though not to slog it out in the line of battle against heavily armoured ships.

A maritime island nation like Britain, with vital, worldwide interests, has always been peculiarly vulnerable to the *guerre de course*, the attack on her merchant shipping on which her life depends. A continental power like France, with a smaller overseas empire and infinitely less at stake on the great ocean highways, has always been obliged to spend more on her army in order to defend her long land frontiers. She could not hope to match the British battle-fleet, nor, after Napoleon's dream of empire faded, did she need to; for her battleships were an expensive luxury, but a few dozen fast, heavily armed cruisers could do great harm to her historic enemy at comparatively little expense. Thus the cruiser became a commerce destroyer as well as a commerce defender, the weapon of both the weaker naval power and the stronger. In the Royal Navy the cruiser had to fulfil both functions, performing her traditional task of protecting the country's merchant marine from interference and at the same time denying the use of the sea to the shipping of her enemies. To a predominantly land power cruiser warfare was a useful secondary form of the offensive. To a maritime power it was often, and of necessity, defensive. But the overall naval superiority afforded by the British battle-fleet, which permitted the British cruisers to range the oceans safeguarding British shipping, also enabled those cruisers to sweep the enemy's shipping from the seas, shutting it up in harbour and stopping the enemy's maritime trade almost completely.

In the twenty years of almost continual hostilities from the French Revolutionary Wars to the Battle of Waterloo (known as the 'Great War' until a much greater arrived in 1914), the Royal Navy applied the tourniquet of blockade, which Captain Mahan so graphically described nearly a century later, in *The Influence of Sea Power on the French Revolution and Empire*, as 'that noiseless pressure on the vitals of France, that compulsion, whose silence, once noted, becomes to the observer the most striking and awful mark of the working of sea power'. The perfect instruments of blockade were the cruisers, in practice usually frigates, fast, handy but well armed, mounting between thirty and forty guns and of 1000 tons displacement. 'The British squadrons, hugging the French coasts and blocking the French arsenals, were the first line of the defence covering British interests from the Baltic to Egypt, the British colonies in the four quarters of the globe, and the British merchantmen which whitened every sea.' The frigates were sustained on station almost indefinitely by store ships stocked with victuals, even occasionally fresh food, but always powder, shot and ships' stores, cordage and spars and canvas and fresh water. The ships were powered by the wind and the muscles of the sailors.

Close blockade was the classic form, the frigates standing inshore, just off the enemy's ports. Over the horizon were the line-of-battle ships, invisible to those on shore, always ready and anxious to bring to battle any ship brave enough to attempt to break the blockade. As Mahan also wrote, 'Those far-distant, storm-beaten ships, upon which the Grand Army never looked, stood between it and the domination of the world.'

By the middle of the nineteenth century the British cruiser was still the wooden frigate, though now steam-powered and screw-driven. When in the early 1860s the American Confederate navy took to commerce raiding, the British Admiralty feared that the new, fast, powerful American cruisers would be as much of a threat to British commerce as were the French. Armour-plate had transformed the battle-fleet but not the cruiser squadrons. The new British cruisers of the 1870s were to be fast but with little canvas, all-steel but with no armour. Although sail was still in favour partly for historical (or sentimental) reasons and partly for the strictly practical reason that the early steam machinery was unreliable, a combination of sail and steam was to become as inconvenient as it was illogical. The rigging took up too much space and created air resistance, and a large crew was required to handle the sails, which meant less room for machinery and coal. For the cruiser, as for any powerful warship, the masts and yards of a sailing vessel were soon seen to be inappropriate.

By the 1880s whole families of cruisers were being built, protected cruisers of the first, second and third classes, and armoured cruisers. The first-class protected cruiser was an ocean-going vessel for commerce raiding or commerce protection, with an armoured steel deck to guard her machinery spaces and magazines. Below the waterline, instead of vertical side armour, protection was afforded by coal bunkers placed along the ship's side, as coal was thought to be a useful shock-absorber, even against a torpedo explosion. The second-class protected cruiser was smaller, intended not for ocean-going cruiser work but for service in narrow waters, while the third-class protected cruiser, even smaller, was employed as a scouting craft for the fleet. The armoured cruiser had vertical side armour and, like the protected cruiser, at least one armoured deck, but her armoured side belt made this type of cruiser in practice merely a second-class, small battleship by the standards of her time. By 1890 improvements in general design, in machinery and in metallurgy began to allow large armoured cruisers to be constructed with correspondingly heavier guns—two, four or even six guns of 9.2-inch calibre, as well as a battery of the new, quick-firing 6-inch.

A good example of this advance was the British Cressey class (1899–1901), which had thicker armour-plate than some of the older battleships. These were certainly a match for the new French armoured cruisers. The Cressey-class cruisers were able to seek out and fight other cruisers without direct support from the battle-fleet, and for a time these powerful new ships seemed destined to take on all the burden of a naval war except the main fleet actions, though there were those who even thought they should take their place in the line. The demand for more armour, heavier guns, greater speed and endurance was bound to mean bigger ships; in the naval arms race the cruiser was following the trend of the battleship, becoming larger, more powerful, more expensive to build, more demanding of manpower.

At about the same time, and for essentially the same reasons, the light cruiser emerged. More powerful than the third-class protected cruiser, she was bigger (3–6000 tons); she mounted heavier guns (often of 6-inch calibre); she was faster (25–30 knots); and, because she was intended to fight other light cruisers in the protection of commerce, she had vertical side armour. Light cruisers in this form proved ideal for work with the battle-fleet as scouts, and, as heavier gun support for the torpedo-boats, they could destroy even the emerging torpedo-boat destroyers. Light cruisers formed the picket line at Jutland, passing information on the enemy's movements to the Commander-in-Chief, shadowing the enemy's battle-fleet and endeavouring to lure him within gun range of the Grand Fleet.

In this respect cruiser tactics had not changed very much since Nelson's time. Indeed, twenty-five years after Jutland it was the heavy cruisers *Norfolk* and *Suffolk* that shadowed the German battleship *Bismarck* in the Denmark Strait. Their classic cruiser characteristics, which enabled them to keep going at high speed in appalling weather, allowed these two ships—outsize scouts, each with a complement of 800—to hang on to the very much larger *Bismarck* for thirty-six hours.

As far as the most important tasks of the cruiser (blockade and counter-blockade) were concerned, the preceding eighty years had been a time not only of continual technological change but also of considerable strategic confusion in the minds of the admirals on whom lay the responsibility of protecting Britain's worldwide sea-borne trade as well as blockading that of the enemy. Close blockade of an enemy's ports had been a feasible undertaking, though an arduous and a difficult one, in the days of sail, and, surprisingly, the doctrine lasted into the twentieth century, although it must have been obvious for many years that the steam-powered cruiser could not be maintained indefinitely off an enemy coast. Steamships were certainly faster than sailing vessels, and they were not dependent on a favourable wind, but the advantages of their speed and operational flexibility rested on bases and coaling stations. Steam cruisers could hardly coal at sea even if suitable colliers had existed, and their reciprocating engines and their boilers required frequent maintenance, which could be done only in harbour; and while the revolution of steam, armour and explosives had enormously enhanced the offensive power of the cruiser, the defences too, particularly those close to an enemy coast, had been transformed. Against blockading cruiser squadrons, flotillas of small, fast, cheap and quickly produced coastal torpedo-boats, moored mines laid in shallow water and off the entrance to his harbours, and long-range heavy coastal artillery would now be ranged. Finally, to this catalogue must be added perhaps the greatest deterrent of all, the submarine, whose value was quickly shown six weeks after the outbreak of war in 1914, when three Cressey-class armoured cruisers were sunk within the hour, by the same U-boat, off the Dutch coast.

So close blockade gave way to distant blockade. British cruisers now patrolled the trade routes to seek out or bottle up the enemy's merchant shipping, and did so to such purpose that the large German merchant fleet quickly ceased to be of any importance. The success of the distant blockade involved the setting up of examination stations to which suspected blockade-runners could be brought, and this in turn required the stopping and searching of all vessels on the high seas, including those of neutral countries, to discover contraband. The imposition of such a form of blockade was bound to arouse the anger of neutral states, as it had done a century earlier in the French Wars and in the suppression of the slave trade, and the United States Government in particular had always rather piously urged that private property on the high seas, even the property of an enemy, should be exempt from capture or destruction. There was some support for this view in Britain too, where the principle of the 'freedom of the seas' was popular in a country long devoted to free trade. Indeed, as early as 1856, in the Declaration of Paris, Britain had abandoned her claim to contraband (here implying goods destined for the enemy) found in neutral ships. At that time the British concern was the outlawing of the privateer, the 'private-enterprise' weapon against merchant shipping that had always plagued the Admiralty. Besides, in the Victorian age of peace and prosperity Britain expected to be magisterially neutral in any of the few wars that might be fought by others at sea. When in 1914 British cruisers once again began to stop and search neutral vessels, there was an outcry loud enough to prompt the release of many neutral ships laden with contraband on the orders of a Government fearful of offending American and Scandinavian opinion.

Naval officers, not surprisingly, thought differently, and even the level-headed Jellicoe wrote, shortly before the Battle of Jutland, 'We could bring the Germans to their knees in three months by the blockade if the Government would face the protests of neutral countries, and take a firm stand and risk a war with the United States, Norway and Sweden.' His successor in command of the Grand Fleet, Beatty, saw the Tenth Cruiser Squadron, which provided the blockading Northern Patrol, as the one unit that could win the war. By then Jellicoe had become less sure, and argued: 'We may cause them a good deal of suffering and discomfort by the blockade, but we shall not win the war by it. The war will not be won until the enemy's armed forces are defeated—certainly on land, and probably at sea—and therefore it is essential to get our troops to France and keep our communications open.' Jellicoe's caution was well founded, for there were other ways of evading the British cruisers, and blockade-runners could sometimes slip through with a cargo of scarce material. On land the same steam engine that had transformed the navy had also transformed inland transport. The railways of Central Europe enabled Germany to import supplies from neutral countries across land frontiers where the writ of patrolling British cruisers could not run.

In parallel with the change in the role of cruisers as the technique of blockade changed, economic and industrial factors wrought a change in attitude towards the counter-blockade. Since the middle of the nineteenth century Britain had become increasingly dependent on imports of food for her growing population and raw materials for her industry. Fifty years earlier French privateers had captured thousands of merchant ships, even in sight of the English coast, but the steam-powered cruiser could now attack swiftly, and there were greater prizes to be taken. Well before the end of that century fears were loudly voiced that the ready supply of cheap food might thereby be severely curtailed in time of war, and that the consequent rise in prices would hit the poor hardest. The spectre of food riots, insurrection even, encouraged the naval lobby, which was to become strident and influential, calling for yet larger new warship construction programmes to counter the threat from France, Russia and the United States. The Admiralty realized that the naval supremacy that permitted British cruisers to blockade a Continental rival did not automatically assure protection against a counter-blockade by enemy cruisers, and that in this counter-blockade Britain would certainly suffer more, having so much more to lose. The British battle-fleet could undoubtedly defeat any other battle-fleet (or even two fleets combined), but the cruisers might not save Britain from starvation. As early as the 1880s and 1890s admirals and shipowners alike had a prophetic vision of the German counter-blockade of the two great wars that were to come, though it was too soon for them to foresee the U–boats that would be used with such success to bring this about.

Of one thing the admirals were certain: the large British cruiser fleet would always have to be much larger if the merchant marine was to be adequately protected in time of war. But confusion about the proper means of employing those cruisers persisted for many years, even into the Second World War. The ideal strategy, in keeping with the offensive tradition of the world's greatest navy, was deemed to be for British cruisers to hunt down the commerce raiders by patrolling the trade routes. This simple but rather impractical notion was blurred in theory and in practice by the simultaneous (but mistaken) assumption that the most likely place for our trade to be attacked was where shipping converged in the approaches to British ports. Plainly, a different strategy, and even perhaps a warship quite unlike a cruiser, would be required to meet the latter threat.

Instead of attempting to 'cover the seas with our cruisers'—as the First Sea Lord had recommended in 1879—the Admiralty might have given more thought to an ancient remedy: convoy.

19 The 'eyes' of the fleet, 1914. The light cruiser HMS Galatea scouted for Beatty at Jutland. Her clean lines proclaim the technological revolution in the generation preceding the First World War.

Convoy is simply a group of merchantmen escorted by warships, but convoy, the admirals said, was not suited to steam vessels because the faster ones would outstrip the rest—masters of steamships being thought to be less disciplined than the captains of the days of sail. The value of convoy over seven centuries, since the reign of King John, was forgotten. Edward III had made convoy compulsory in war; the treasure ships of Imperial Spain had sailed home in convoy and none was ever taken. Thereafter the convoy system had been in force in time of war for English, French and Dutch merchantmen—with the blessing of Lloyds' underwriters. In the Great War with revolutionary and then Napoleonic France, the convoy system was so successful that in 1798 Parliament made it compulsory.

Merchantmen sailed in large fleets, escorted by sloops and frigates and supported by line-of-battle ships. The steam-powered cruiser had, it was held, somehow invalidated all this accumulated experience of maritime war, since she could attack from any quarter. All that could be done, it seemed, was to advise ships' masters about the safest route to sail, to urge them to report attack to the nearest Royal Navy cruiser and to run, if chased, in order to make the raider burn up more of his coal! By 1905 the Admiralty had almost proposed something like convoy for some ships on busy routes by recommending 'voluntary group sailings' on routes such as that from Gibraltar to England. This measure recognized that a stream of independently sailed vessels gave a raider several good chances of a prize, but that a group of vessels might well escape his attentions, since he was less likely to sight one group of ships than the same number of vessels spread along a trade route. The Admiralty had rediscovered one of the basic principles of the convoy system, but no naval escort was to be provided. Instead, cruisers would be stationed at intervals along the trade routes, ready to go to the aid of the victims. Cruisers were deemed to be better employed in offensive sweeps—much the same remedy that was later offered to counter the U-boats in the wars of the twentieth century.

Ironically, this mental block was overcome in the Admiralty's acceptance of escorted convoy as appropriate for colliers and storeships servicing the fleet, and for troopships. The battle-fleet itself, it may be observed, always sailed as a rather special convoy, escorted by cruisers and torpedo-boat destroyers. The convoy argument is still alive and well today, despite its long history and undoubted success in the two world wars.

By 1914 the emphasis on the battle-fleet in both British and German navies had bred two main types of cruiser, the fast, well armed and lightly armoured scout for fleet work and the very large armoured cruiser. The triple revolution in naval gunnery, armour and propulsion which led to the *Dreadnought* battleship also led to a new cruiser concept, that of the battle-cruiser. By 1914 the battle-cruiser had a speed nearer that of a light cruiser, 25 knots and more, which gave her a useful margin over the 21-knot battleship. She mounted a battleship's guns, but her armour was much thinner and her high speed, of course, required more machinery space. So designed, the battle-cruiser was well able to catch and destroy the commerce-raiding cruiser, but, strangely, this was done only once in the First World War. In 1914 Admiral Graf Spee's cruiser squadron was off the Pacific coast of South America, where he was found by Admiral Cradock with two less powerful armoured cruisers. Cradock's small squadron was destroyed, only a light cruiser escaping, but revenge was a matter of a few weeks away. The Admiralty dispatched three battle-cruisers, one to guard the West Indies should Admiral Graf Spee pass through the Panama Canal (the United States then being neutral) and two, *Invincible* and *Inflexible*, to the Falkland Islands, which the German admiral was expected to attack. It was there that Graf Spee's squadron was defeated and the armoured cruisers *Scharnhorst* and *Gneisenau* were sunk. Thereafter, the British battle-cruisers

20 'Heavy cavalry', 1941. Between the wars the heavy cruiser was in demand in every navy. HMS Kenya *mounted twelve 6-inch guns.*

returned to the North Sea, where they were to be employed with the battle-fleet. *Invincible* herself was destroyed in the Battle of Jutland.

It was left to the Germans to fulfil another long-held expectation of the battle-cruiser. For many years before this war the Admiralty had feared the fast French cruisers that might slip across the Channel to bombard undefended English coastal towns—though what military or economic purpose would thereby be served no one thought to ask. Few people considered how slight the damage would be that could be inflicted by such swift and short bombardments; and indeed when the German battle-cruisers made good the threat in the First World War, attacking towns on the north-east coast, so it proved. The shelling of undefended English towns was, of course, a device to lure the British battle-cruisers into pursuit and destruction, it was hoped, by the High Seas Fleet, while the Grand Fleet's battleships could be ambushed by submarines outside their bases. Insignificant though these bombardments were, they caused great embarrassment to the Admiralty, although it had never been claimed that the Royal Navy could prevent them.

21 One of the most attractive ships ever built, but the battle-cruiser compared poorly with the fast battleship. HMS Renown *was too late for Jutland, and her sister ship was sunk with* Prince of Wales *in 1941.*

At Jutland both German and British fleets had scouting forces of light cruisers and battle-cruisers. (The British armoured cruisers proved an expensive failure: three had been torpedoed in September 1914, two sunk by German cruisers soon after and three swiftly destroyed at Jutland.) The battle-cruisers were intended to smash the light cruisers screening the enemy fleet and to maintain contact with the enemy while denying him information, but they were also to fight their own kind in a miniature fleet action, taking station in the van of the battle-fleet. Sir David Beatty's battle-cruiser squadron comprised six battle-cruisers and attendant light forces; Admiral Hipper's First Scouting Group was composed of five battle-cruisers. Beatty's superiority was quickly reversed when two of his ships were destroyed in spectacular fashion, with horrifying loss of life. It was then that Beatty made his famous observation, 'There's something wrong with our bloody ships today,' a view he was to express again after the battle, adding, 'and something wrong with our system.'

The battle-cruiser had been the first love of Admiral Fisher, not the *Dreadnought* he also conceived. When recalled to the Admiralty at the start of the First World War, Fisher still insisted that the formula for victory at sea was speed and long-range artillery; he gave much less thought to fire control, fleet communications and protection. Under his direction work was begun on some huge battle-cruisers: *Courageous* and *Glorious*, mounting four 15-inch guns, and *Furious*, designed for two 18-inch guns (which we met earlier, in chapter three). These ships were intended for Fisher's favourite plan, an attack on Germany's Baltic coast in support of a landing by British or Russian troops. Fisher's scheme did not survive his tenure of office, but some of the smaller ships and the three battle-cruisers were completed. The two 15-inch-gun ships *Courageous* and *Glorious* joined the fleet in 1917, but *Furious* commissioned with only one great gun, not two. *Courageous* and *Glorious*, with their long, unprotected sides, were doomed to failure as large cruisers if they ever had to fight other battle-cruisers. Three more battle-cruisers were completed: *Repulse* and *Renown*, which joined the fleet after the Battle of Jutland, and *Hood* after the war, in 1920 (she was to have been the first of four great ships, but she alone was completed). The largest battle-cruiser of her time at 42,000 tons, *Hood* was also the largest warship afloat until the Washington Treaty expired. The Second World War was upon her before she could be modernized, and she blew up after a chance but vital hit in the magazine—in much the same way as the battle-cruisers at Jutland—when she took on the infinitely more powerful and better designed *Bismarck*.

A few months later *Repulse*, also unmodernized, was to fight gallantly but vainly against the bombs and torpedoes of the Japanese naval air force, and *Renown* alone survived the war.

None of these three British battle-cruisers had proved fit to engage a modern battleship. Although they could have dealt with a 'pocket battleship' or armoured cruiser, they were no match for the new and very powerful German battle-cruisers *Scharnhorst* and *Gneisenau* (successors to their namesakes of 1914), which were, in effect, fast battleships. Between the wars the concept was adopted elsewhere, three of Japan's four battle-cruisers being reconstructed as fast battleships. Then, in the Second World War, when the battle-cruiser was already an historical curiosity—and when the battleship herself had yielded pride of place to the aircraft-carrier—the United States built her first (and last) pair of battle-cruisers, *Alaska* and *Guam*. Although only lightly armoured, these ships were far better protected by internal subdivision and modern damage-control systems. Their 12-inch guns were a reminder of the very first battle-cruiser, *Invincible*; forty years on, however, radar and rapid fire made them much more powerful weapons.

Between the two world wars the Royal Navy's cruiser strength (around fifty and increasing) was greater than that of any other power, although at the Washington and, later, the London Naval Conference the United States contested this superiority. The Admiralty claimed that as many as seventy cruisers were needed to protect the widely scattered British colonies and dependencies, now at their most extensive, and to safeguard the even larger informal empire of British commercial interests by patrolling the trade routes to protect the huge British merchant marine. Even though the most serious threat to maritime trade in the recent war had come not from the enemy's surface raiders but from his submarines, the Admiralty was less concerned about the possible recurrence of that danger than it was about commerce raiding by cruisers and auxiliaries. To the Admiralty a very strong cruiser force was essential.

Indeed, so many cruisers were considered to be required for these tasks that the Admiralty concluded that large numbers of auxiliary, armed merchant cruisers would again be needed. The 1914–18 blockade of Germany had imposed a great strain on the Royal Navy, as it had in the French Wars a hundred years earlier. Armed merchant cruisers (mostly requisitioned passenger liners) were a cheap means of augmenting cruiser strength. Although they were fast, they were armed only with a few 6-inch guns and were quite unprotected. They were a deathtrap if brought to surface action, as proved to be the case for the brave ships' companies of *Rawalpindi* and *Jervis Bay* in the Second World War.

While the Washington Treaty imposed a limit on battleship size, cruisers actually *increased* in tonnage because designers found themselves building up to, and often above, the Treaty limit. The new 8-inch gun was to make the heavy cruiser a formidable unit, but it was difficult to pack four large twin turrets, together with some armour protection, the means for achieving high speed and great endurance for ocean work and a ship's company of 800, inside 10,000 tons. Indeed, most navies were also re-equipping with heavy cruisers mounting broadsides of eight, twelve or even fifteen 6-inch guns. The scale of the cruiser programmes in the 1930s is clearly shown in the following table of their strength.

	BRITISH AND COMMONWEALTH	USA	JAPAN	ITALY	GERMANY
1932	52	19	27	17	3
1939	62	32	39	21	11

The cruiser had long been essentially a gunboat, though much larger, faster and more powerful than the sloop and the river gunboat. 'Cruizers' (as they were then known) as well as gunboats carried the burden of the fifty years' patrolling on the West Africa station to suppress the slave trade and patrolled the Persian Gulf in search of slavers and pirates even into the twentieth century. A cruiser could move quickly to meet any threat to the peace and security of a colony or dependency. She had a ship's company large enough to be able to land a sizeable detachment of bluejackets and marines and was roomy enough to carry a battalion or more of soldiers in reasonable comfort. The cruiser was truly a mobile imperial police station, and as instrument of gunboat diplomacy she was ideal, mounting enough heavy artillery to present a real force, large and imposing enough to appear as a credible extension of national will, but not so large as to present a greater threat than foreign policy demanded. So, in the twentieth century, as the great powers became more numerous and as European rivalries were projected right around the globe, the gunboat and the sloop gradually gave place to the cruiser as the appropriate platform for a senior naval officer who was not merely an imperial policeman but also, even more, a pro-consular representative of his Government. A good example of this extended role was presented during the Japanese invasion of China in the 1930s, when British and American cruisers were deployed on station to inspire confidence and credibility in the British or American guarantees of protection to their traders and missionaries. The earlier river gunboats would not have carried enough weight in this larger context.

The cruiser on the China station, in the South Atlantic or, in earlier years, off the Great Banks in support of the Fisheries Protection Squadron might be away from her home port for three years, the ship's company remaining together throughout the commission. The transport of mail to distant foreign stations took three weeks each way (even to the Mediterranean it took a week). There were no wives on station, and officers and sailors alike were content making their own fun with sport and games, pulling and sailing regattas and 'runs ashore' in strange places— all of which generated among the crew a remarkably close sense of identity with each ship and with the squadron or fleet to which she belonged.

The typical Washington Treaty heavy cruiser was a big ship. Like the battleship, she was well found, with her own workshops and all the resources and utilities of a small town, and the 10,000-miles range of the heavy cruiser in most navies made her truly ocean-going. Although the cruiser was nearing the end of her traditional role by 1939, she was about to enter her most active and strenuous period since the wars with France.

Once again, trade protection was the chief task of the British cruiser force and trade destruction the task of the relatively few German cruisers. These at once began the *guerre de course*, when two 'pocket battleships', *Graf Spee* and *Deutschland*, were loose in the Atlantic. To quote Roskill, the official historian:

> The general policy [of the Admiralty] was to patrol the focal areas with cruisers, to form ocean convoys in particularly dangerous waters or for the most valuable ships, but, in general, to rely on 'evasive routing' of shipping from one focal area to the next, at any rate until such time as escorts for ocean convoys were available. When the presence of a raider was known or strongly suspected hunting groups were immediately to be formed.

In eighty years Admiralty thinking had altered little and was still equivocal about convoy. Merchantmen would be escorted only in 'particularly dangerous waters' or if they were 'the most valuable ships'; cruisers would patrol 'focal areas'; but an organized convoy system over the long sea lanes was not at once put into force. When the 'pocket battleships' were known to be at large, eight 'hunting groups' were quickly formed from twenty British and French cruisers, battleships, battle-cruisers and aircraft-carriers to deal with *Graf Spee* and *Deutschland*.

The South American division, comprising the large heavy cruiser *Exeter* and the smaller *Ajax* and *Achilles*, was one such group and had an early success, intercepting *Graf Spee* nine weeks later. This was a remarkable tribute to the Force Commander, Commodore Harwood, who, acting on a hunch and entirely on his own initiative, concentrated his squadron where he had decided that *Graf Spee*'s captain would appear next, 'tempted by the rich pickings of the traffic off Rio de Janeiro and the River Plate'. Harwood's strategic difficulties were formidable. The South Atlantic is a vast ocean, and he had to watch for all enemy ships, merchantmen as well as raiders, besides patrolling his 'focal areas'. Hunting a 'pocket battleship', whose 11-inch guns were heavier and could outrange those of his own ships, was a daunting task, and it was not made easier by the lack of reliable information about enemy movements or by false distress messages originated by the enemy. By far his gravest weakness was the absence of a fast fleet oiler to replenish his own ships at sea. The problem was well understood by the naval staff: a common peacetime exercise in the classrooms of the Royal Navy had required the interception (on paper, showing the necessary dispositions) of an enemy commerce raider, in which particular attention was paid to the endurance of the pursuing British cruisers and the location of fuel supplies. The distance from the River Plate to Port Stanley in the Falkland Islands, the nearest British base, was 1000 miles; a man-of-war's access to a neutral port in wartime was restricted by the Hague Convention to once in three months. Harwood's 'hunting group' might run short of fuel, but his quarry would not, for *Graf Spee* had her own attendant tanker, as did almost every German commerce raider. The Admiralty's inability to make similar provision was matched by its reluctance to accept that ocean convoys should be formed at the outbreak of war and the ships deployed as 'hunting groups' should be used instead as escorts. Roskill records, by way of explanation for this judgement, that the sixty British and Dominion cruisers available were considered too few for ocean convoy to be possible. Harwood's Commander-in-Chief in the

South Atlantic disposed of eight cruisers, four of them twenty years old, and if these were indeed insufficient for ocean convoy, they must have seemed an even more inadequate force for the exacting duties of searching the vast South Atlantic and patrolling 'focal areas'.

As often in war, flaws in strategic planning were to be redeemed in battle by the skill and bravery of Harwood and his force—and some good fortune. In general, German surface raiders avoided naval action, not for want of courage but because their whole purpose was to continue to pose as a threat in being and thus to pin down much larger Allied naval forces which would have been more usefully employed elsewhere, and even commerce raiding was secondary to that main aim. Harwood's own strategy was faultless: he chose the battle-ground and brought his enemy to action. His tactics are also worthy of note. He well knew that none of his three ships was a match for *Graf Spee*; even her secondary armament of 5.9-inch guns was quite equal to the main battery of 6-inch mounted by *Ajax* and *Achilles*; while *Exeter*'s 8-inch pieces were still small compared with the modern 11-inch guns of *Graf Spee*. Harwood had already worked out his battle plan, which was to split his force, so that the enemy would either have to neglect one opponent or divide his fire between two. After ninety minutes *Exeter* was out of the fight, heavily damaged, but the two smaller cruisers, firing as one, continued the action until *Graf Spee* declined to finish the unequal contest and retreated towards the River Plate, where her captain sought refuge in the neutral port of Montevideo. Shortly afterwards he scuttled his ship rather than emerge to face what he wrongly believed was a strong British squadron, including a battle-cruiser, waiting outside.

Even during the years of massive cruiser strength, a rival had appeared: the aeroplane. Shortly after the First World War long-range, shore-based aircraft began seriously to compete with cruisers for ocean reconnaissance, and even before that war Admiral Fisher had written, 'Aviation will *surely* supplant cruisers.' The process took longer than it might have done, partly because of the technical difficulties attending naval aviation, partly because in most navies the proper uses of aircraft were imperfectly understood, and partly because in some countries control of naval aviation was vested in a separate air force, whose chief concern was 'strategic' bombing of the enemy's homeland rather than maritime war. But for all these reasons, which might together be termed the 'state of the art', by 1939 Fisher's prognosis was nowhere near reality. Through the early years of the Second World War and until the tide turned in favour of the Allies in the Pacific, the Royal Navy demanded ever greater exertions from its cruiser force.

The war was to prove for these ships, and for those of the Americans too, a severe test of cruiser strength and cruiser doctrine. As in the previous conflict, British cruisers enforced the blockade of Germany (once again, distant blockade) with armed merchant cruisers to reinforce the patrol line. British cruisers fought offensively to disrupt the supply route across the Mediterranean to the effective and at first successful German-Italian army fighting in North Africa, and defensively, escorting convoys to the beleaguered garrison of Malta, as well as supporting the army in Norway, Greece and Crete. Half a world away, in the Java Sea, *Exeter*, one of the victors of the River Plate, fought her last gallant action in a cruiser battle against the Japanese. Some of the fiercest and bloodiest naval battles ever were to be fought between American and Japanese cruisers in the waters off Guadalcanal in the South Pacific. In these night actions, as most surface engagements had become, fire would be opened at a range of 2 or 3 miles, and sometimes less than 1 mile, when one force surprised another. These cruiser-to-cruiser actions, in which battleships and destroyers sometimes took part, were an unexpected return to the kind of naval warfare that had long been thought out of date, with searchlights suddenly lighting up the target and heavy guns firing at point-blank range. Radar had not yet supplanted the old-fashioned skills of seamanship and gunnery. Such fierce sea fights had more in common with naval battles of the seventeenth and eighteenth centuries, as witness the official historian's description of the last hours of USS *Atlanta*, sunk off Guadalcanal on Friday, 13 November 1942:

> Their ship was ravaged by more than fifty large-caliber shell hits, holed by torpedoes and consumed by fire. Survivors found devastation behind every bulkhead and in almost every compartment. Below decks men groped in complete darkness through acrid smoke and sloshed heavily in oily waters on flooded decks. Cursing and coughing, they labored to seal hull ruptures, succor the many wounded and bring fires under control. The main deck was a charnel house. Burned and eviscerated corpses, severed limbs and chunks of flesh mixed with steel debris littered it from stem to stern.

Such actions in the South Pacific were closely connected with the equally bitter struggle being waged on shore and in the air. The cruisers fought in support of land operations, bombarding enemy coastal defences, protecting troopships and landing craft, escorting the army's seaborne supplies. The fleet and the armies shared a common strategy not only in the Pacific but also in the Mediterranean and in north-west Europe, where large-scale land operations required sea power to ensure the landing of the troops and their subsequent supply and support. Even cruisers engaged in support of convoys to northern Russia were fighting in the same battle as the armies they helped to sustain. The Russian convoys were a nightmare, even for the cruisers and the other heavy ships that sailed in support of the close escort of the merchantmen. Mountainous seas, freezing spray and winter gales battered the ships for many days and nights, and in those northern latitudes the summer night gave no cloak to the convoy, while in winter they sailed on in perpetual darkness and gloom. The cruiser could and did drive off the enemy's heavy surface ships, and her fire-power was useful in helping to break up the formations of attacking aircraft; but already she was taking second place to the escort carrier. The march of technology demanded a change in the cruiser's role, but it was to be a long time before she re-emerged, armed with missiles and helicopters, as an anti-aircraft *and* anti-submarine ship.

If the aircraft had become the cruiser's rival as a scout, it had also become her most dangerous enemy. The German light cruiser *Königsberg* was its first victim in 1940, and in the Second World War one-third of British and Commonwealth cruiser losses were from air attack—two were sunk by bombing in the withdrawal from Crete, and six others severely damaged. The American experience was different: of nine cruisers lost, five were sunk by (mainly) cruiser gunfire, two by submarine torpedoes, one by destroyer torpedo attack and only one by aerial torpedoes. A duel not unlike that between armour and the gun had begun—and it still continues—between the surface ship and the strike aircraft. Even before the Second World War some of the older British light cruisers were converted to anti-aircraft ships, and a new class was built, mounting dual-purpose artillery. The cruiser proved an ideal anti-aircraft gun platform, being steadier than the smaller escort vessels. She could also keep up with the carrier strike fleets at high speed; her tall masts could carry more fire-control radar; her magazines could hold more ammunition; and her considerable battery of large-calibre anti-aircraft guns was also effective against other ships and for bombarding shore targets. At the end of the war the cruiser seemed to have an assured future as part of a fast carrier task force, functioning as platform for radar-controlled anti-aircraft guns, and many such vessels were entering service in the world's navies.

22 White elephant or super-gunboat? Seventy-five years after the first battle cruiser, the Soviet navy acquires Kirov, 32,000 tons, on which heavy guns are replaced by missile-launchers.

By the 1960s, rocket-propelled guided missiles went to sea in quantity, and there were those who held that there was no more room in navies for a heavy-gun cruiser firing a large quantity of ammunition if the same kill rate could be achieved by one guided missile, particularly as this new weapon could also be fitted in a much smaller ship. As is so often found with new devices of all sorts, the arguments are not as clear, nor the right conclusions as easy to reach, as this stark choice might suggest. Guns, certainly big ones, are difficult and expensive to manufacture, heavy to install and complicated to operate, while a missile launcher is relatively cheap, light and simple. But the shell is cheap and easy to make by comparison with the missile, which is extremely expensive, complicated and difficult to produce. (To put this in some perspective, a surface-to-air guided missile costs about a thousand times as much as an anti-aircraft shell.) It is clearly not sensible to use such an expensive weapon if the cheaper gun will do the job or, indeed, if the operational situation is better suited to gunfire than missiles. Thus, both the gun and the missile are still to be found in nearly all larger warships the world over.

But the guided missile became the ideal weapon for those navies that did not possess the resources to deploy big ships, much less aircraft-carriers. One fast patrol boat fitted with surface-to-surface guided missiles could deliver a greater punch to a longer range than a cruiser's broadside and, moreover, was almost certain to hit. For the Soviet navy in the 1950s, at that time still very much a coast-defence force, the guided missile was the obvious weapon to put to sea; like the coastal submarine, the fast patrol boat may be seen as a modern version of the early torpedo-boat of a century ago. To counter the threat of the long-range projection of force by the numerous American aircraft-carriers, the Soviet navy then had only its shore-based aircraft and its ocean-going submarines, but without carriers, the Northern Fleet clearly needed more than missile-armed, offshore fast patrol boats. In the Norwegian Sea and beyond, the requirement was for vessels of greater endurance, able to keep the sea in bad weather and big enough to mount a formidable battery of surface-to-surface missile launchers and the necessary radar guidance systems. Thus the large guided-missile destroyer or cruiser achieved its place in the new ocean-going Soviet navy, the astounding expansion of which started as late as 1962.

If one response to the American aircraft-carrier was the Soviet missile-armed large destroyer or cruiser, the counter to that in turn was still to be the carrier-borne aircraft. In both the American and British navies the technology of naval aviation had been perfected and was widely available, so it seemed un-necessary to spend resources on anti-ship missiles when high-performance aircraft were there to do the same job and when most of their efforts were concentrated on anti-submarine warfare. When the decision was taken in 1966 to build no more large fleet carriers for the Royal Navy, a yawning 'missile gap' at once became apparent. With a lead-time for the development of advanced weapons systems of ten years, even the resources of Western technology could not close this gap quickly; but, after staggering expenditure, this has now been done. The 'platforms' (as it is now fashionable to call warships) that emerged have become large ships, as they have in the Soviet navy. They must be big enough to keep the sea, with long endurance, high speed and room to mount what are by now large missile-launchers and several reloads of their large missiles, in addition to radar arrays and one or two helicopters. Thus in the US Navy ships designated as destroyers or frigates are now typically as large as cruisers of the Second World War. The apparent confusion of nomenclature, although tiresome and even misleading, is not new, as we have noted; a century and more ago the frigate was becoming the cruiser, and she was, in the form of HMS *Warrior*, actually superior to the battleship of her day. For a cruiser-size vessel to be called a frigate seems strange only in the twentieth century. The frigate returned to sea in the 1940s as a destroyer-size anti-submarine vessel and since then has generally been a type of anti-submarine and anti-aircraft escort destroyer. Until the development of the modern sonar and especially of the helicopter, with its dipping sonar and its anti-submarine guided missiles, the cruiser was ill-suited to anti-submarine warfare. Today to keep on station in the Norwegian Sea or the Denmark Strait an anti-submarine escort needs the size and endurance of at least a small cruiser if she is to provide a useful platform for all those functions just described. As their weapons have grown, so we have seen the appearance of very large escorts for this role, often bigger than the cruisers built between the wars. It is, in short, not the name by which she is known but the function that she performs that allows almost any warship to be considered a 'cruiser' today.

In spite of various alarms and excursions, history shows that in one important respect the cruiser has not matched up to expectations. Since the emergence of the steam-powered cruiser in the mid-nineteenth century, she has achieved remarkably little as a commerce raider or, indeed, as an enforcer of blockade; against maritime nations like Britain and Japan she has been far outclassed by the submarine. The cruiser's role as the 'eyes' of the fleet and as long-range ocean patrol has largely disappeared now that long-range maritime reconnaissance is conducted by aircraft and by satellite photography. So far has the trend moved away from the cruiser type that large and important navies, like the Royal Navy, have virtually abandoned the concept. In a navy which does not have fast carrier battle groups the anti-aircraft cruiser is not required, nor will there be much need, in the foreseeable future, for cruisers to bombard enemy shore defences. However, for this residual purpose the US Navy began the development of the lightweight 8-inch gun as the previous generation of heavy-gun cruisers ended their lives, but such bombardment is now much more of a gunboat task (as off the coasts of Vietnam) than a wartime function, and certainly the latter-day gunboat and 'flag-showing' duties of the cruiser can equally well be undertaken by the guided missile destroyer, detached from a task group.

So this is the cruiser (whatever she may be called) of today. At 10,000 tons displacement, she is about the size of a heavy cruiser of the Second World War, though her complement, 440 officers and men, is less than half that of the heavy cruiser. She mounts a variety of anti-submarine missiles and carries two helicopters. Her magazines store eighty surface-to-air missiles; eventually she is to have the Tomahawk cruise missile as well. Only in guns does she appear inferior to her recent ancestors, but the two 5-inch semi-automatic mountings are powerful weapons indeed. She is a guided-missile cruiser, fast and, because of her nuclear power plant, of unlimited range. Sometimes deployed by the US Sixth Fleet, such ships are usually in company with one of the great nuclear-powered fleet carriers like *Nimitz* and a small battle group of frigates and destroyers with their fleet train of supply ships. In this context the cruiser of today has primarily defensive duties—air defence, and anti-submarine work. Yet patrolling for months on end, thousands of miles from her home port, she is a true descendant of the cruiser of Nelson's day. Even in her latest role she performs tasks that would be readily understood, in principle, by the admirals and captains sailing in those same waters two centuries ago.

Chapter Seven

SUBMARINE

The submarine is not an honest weapon. It suggests the foot pad, the garotte, and the treacherous knife dug in an opponent's back when he is off-guard.

SIR ARCHIBALD HURD, 1902

Six thirty on the morning of 22 September 1914. The Great European War is only six weeks old. The Seventh Cruiser Squadron—the armoured cruisers *Aboukir*, *Cressey* and *Hogue*—on patrol in the North Sea off the Dutch coast, is sighted by the German submarine U9 (Lieutenant-Commander Otto Weddigen). The U-boat aims a torpedo at the leading ship, *Aboukir*. She sinks in twenty-five minutes, but the senior officer, Captain Drummond of *Aboukir*, has ordered his two consorts to close in order to rescue survivors. Within the hour all three ships have been sunk. Of 2200 officers and men, 1459 drown. The submarine has gone to war.

The idea is very old, as old as the line-of-battle ship, but practicable underwater craft had to wait upon the development of marine engineering. From 1880 progress was especially rapid in France and the United States, and a few underwater craft were built for the French navy, but as an effective vessel of war the submarine did not emerge until the turn of the century. Best-known perhaps, though she was not the first, is the Holland submersible. Her designer, an Irishman, had conceived such a craft as a secret weapon for use against Britain in the Fenian cause. After some years of financial difficulty and quarrels with fellow Irishmen, Holland sold his latest designs to the US Navy, and one year later, in 1901, the Royal Navy acquired its first submarine, a Holland boat (all submarines are called 'boats') built under licence by Vickers at Barrow in Furness. Sixty-three feet long, displacing 120 tons under water, she had a crew of nine and one torpedo tube. Underwater she could make 5 knots, but on the surface she was driven by a petrol engine at 8 knots. Most modern submarines look remarkably like that early Holland boat in outline.

The submarine is unique among sea vessels. No other ship can sink completely and then return to the surface. She can flood her tanks with sea water to submerge and then blow the water out of the tanks by means of compressed air to resurface, but if she goes too deep, the water pressure will crush her hull. In the unique condition of 'neutral buoyancy' (neither heavier nor lighter than the water she displaces), a submarine can 'hover' underwater by emptying or flooding her 'trimming tanks' and by using her hydroplanes (essentially horizontal rudders, like an aircraft's ailerons) at each end of the boat. When on the surface, the first submarines were driven by petrol engines, but the risk of explosion and fire was so great that diesel motors were substituted. Both of these oil-burning engines need fresh air, however, so when submerged the boat was powered by electric motors. The batteries for these motors were (and still are) very large, but they required recharging frequently under their heavy load, and the submarine had to surface to use her diesel engines to do this. The early boats could stay down perhaps twenty-four hours, less if under way, but the air soon became too foul for the crew to breathe. For short spurts a submarine could manage 7 or 8 knots submerged, but 3 to 5 knots was a realistic speed, and she spent most of her time, on patrol or on passage, on the surface.

23 Britain's first submarine, a Holland boat (1901).

Design went ahead quickly, and by the outbreak of the First World War submarine performance was impressive, with diesel engines which could take a boat across the Atlantic and back. The submarine had arrived in good time to mate with the torpedo. The torpedo was at first launched from the torpedo-boat, but once the technique of expelling it by compressed air from the submerged hull of a submarine was mastered, a new weapons system had been born. It is not altogether surprising that in the experimental early years before the First World War the most suitable employment for this new device was not immediately obvious to navies reared on the battleship doctrine. Some naval officers thought of it as a variant of the coast-defence torpedo-boat; their general idea was that submarines would lie in wait for the approach of an enemy fleet, and when some great battleship came within range their torpedoes would strike without warning, and they would slip away unnoticed.

To naval officers trained to think offensively, coast defence was of less importance than the decisive encounter of rival battle-fleets. They held that the submarine was too slow to work with the fleet—as indeed she was (even for coastal defence) unless by chance she was favourably placed in the path of an enemy warship. Even on the surface the submarine could not move quickly to another target. The torpedo itself was still slow and notoriously unreliable, and although by 1914 a range of 3 or 4 miles might be attained, this was still very short for its purpose, and the *effective* range was much less. To carry out a successful attack the submarine had to be ahead of her target; to see it the captain had to use his periscope, and his horizon was very short. At such shallow depth his boat was vulnerable to gunfire or even to being rammed (as some actually were). If these hazards were successfully overcome, the attack might still fail because the compressed air which drove the torpedoes made a highly visible trail of bubbles on the surface, and the ship attacked could turn towards them, sharply narrowing the target area. This man-oeuvre, endlessly practised, was called 'combing the track'.

The loss of the armoured cruisers *Aboukir*, *Cressey* and *Hogue* early in the war abruptly engendered a healthy respect for the submarine, even among its most vocal critics. After this dramatic success and other similar exploits by German and British submarine captains, the pendulum swung hard the other way, and most fleet commanders developed an exaggerated fear of the offensive capacity of the new weapon. They had some reason to do so, for the submarine achieved much—and very quickly. For a time British submarine captains dominated parts of the Baltic and the Sea of Marmara beyond the Dardanelles, and the German U-boats sufficiently alarmed the Commander-in-Chief of the Grand Fleet to drive him from his anchorages and indeed, for a time, out of the North Sea altogether. In 1914 the great natural fleet anchorage of Scapa Flow in the Orkneys was still undefended against this threat. (Scapa Flow's defences were actually penetrated twenty-five years later, when the battleship *Royal Oak* was sunk by a U-boat, with great loss of life.) An officer in Sir David Beatty's battle-cruiser fleet wrote, 'We are hunted about the sea and have nowhere to rest.'

Most fleet commanders were unsure of what the submarine could do, though it seemed possible to them that the submarine captain could intercept a battle-fleet at high speed in order to place himself in the ideal torpedo-firing position, ahead of the ships. There is no doubt that it was this fear of a submarine trap that made Sir John Jellicoe extremely cautious in his pursuit of the High Seas Fleet. These fears were strongly reinforced when in the Dogger Bank action of 1915 Beatty claimed that he and his staff had sighted submarine periscopes in the path of his battle-cruisers, although if they were there, no attack resulted. The submarine had thus achieved, remarkably quickly, the classic aim of the fleet in being by presenting a threat far beyond her actual capacity and so hampering the commander of a vastly superior surface fleet by making him over-cautious. In the event, although several pre-*Dreadnought* battleships were torpedoed in the First World War, no dreadnought was lost to a U-boat. Even in the Second World War, pitted against improved submarines and torpedoes, only two battleships—*Barham* and the Japanese *Kongo*—were torpedoed and sunk *at sea* by a submarine, although many other types of warship were to be victims.

The submarine threat to a fleet of warships, based though it was on a misunderstanding of what was possible, encouraged most admirals to see the submarine as an underwater torpedo-boat, which she was, and as a flotilla craft, which she was not. Every navy of size and importance was built around the battle-fleet, created and maintained almost solely to fight the decisive action against the enemy battle-fleet. The battleship's big guns constituted the principal weapons system, and all other forms of naval warfare, all other weapons systems, were merely ancillary. The battle-fleet was screened by squadrons of cruisers, the purpose of which was to scout and to deal with the enemy's scouting forces, and by flotillas of torpedo-boat destroyers, whose function was to drive off enemy torpedo-boat attacks and to attack the enemy battle-fleet with torpedoes. To these forces, they thought, would be added the flotilla of fast fleet submarines, disposed on the flank as a submarine trap from which the enemy would turn away, only to blunder into gun range of the battle-fleet. In the First World War, initially at the insistence of Admiral Fisher, designs took shape for a variety of strange submersible craft to fill this role. The 'K' class boats, steam-driven and capable of 23 knots on the surface, were intended to be submersible destroyers. They proved awkward to handle, especially as the steam plant had to be shut down when the craft was preparing to dive, and they were dangerous to serve in. They were ill-suited to high-speed work with the fleet, and in darkness they were all too likely to be rammed by their own side. Undismayed, the Admiralty continued to build a series of experimental craft in the fashion of submersible cruisers and even aircraft-carriers. There was also a monitor submarine, mounting one 12-inch gun, though it should have been obvious that without a fire-control system and with only one gun, accurate shooting was not possible. Much the same might have been said of the 'cruiser' submarine, mounting four 5.25-inch guns, had she to engage an enemy cruiser, and equally impractical was the aircraft-carrying submarine, which would merely have advertised her presence by the appearance of her seaplane in the neighbourhood of enemy shipping. The notion of submarines fighting each other under the sea was also realized as early as 1918 in the submarine-hunting boats of the British 'R' class—some of the very few boats that were faster under water (15 knots) than on the surface (9.5 knots)—though they had no accurate means of detecting, much less locating, other sub-marines, and it could hardly have been supposed that such craft should battle blindly with each other underwater. All the same, although these experimental designs for submarine monitors, cruisers and aircraft-carriers were all built, they were seldom repeated.

It is all the more surprising that the idea of the submarine as a fleet warship persisted between the two world wars and even well into the second. The submarine was considered well able to work in flotillas and to take part in fleet operations, and in the 1920s the Japanese did not think it fanciful to assign the submarine to the attack on Pearl Harbor when this was first planned. It was several years later that the aircraft-carriers were included, and in the event submarines did attack—with no success—while the aircraft achieved a dramatic victory. In the Japanese advance on Midway, in June 1942, the admiral commanding submarines actually sailed in one of his boats, as the flag officer of a squadron of battleships or cruisers might have, but, not surprisingly, he remained entirely ignorant of the course of the battle and could do nothing to influence the part played by his submarines. The Japanese navy thought the submarine should be employed only against enemy warships; the mistake was to cost it many lost opportunities. There were successes as well as failures. Of the sixteen American and British aircraft-carriers lost in the Second World War, four were sunk by German and two by Japanese submarines, while *Yorktown*, off Midway, was finished off by a submarine, having been crippled by the bombs and torpedoes of Japanese carrier-borne aircraft. Operational experience showed that, whether deployed as one of a flotilla in company with the fleet or independently on a patrol line, the submarine captain was usually lucky to find himself in the ideal firing position for a torpedo attack on a fast-moving warship. There were other, easier targets in abundance.

Here we turn back the pages of the history of this sinister new weapons system to trace some other lines of its evolution, noting first, perhaps, that from its earliest days the submarine branch was always somewhat separate from the rest of the Service. It is fair to say that this was a consequence more of custom and the attitude of both submariners and officers in general service than of any official edict. Most sailors are by nature conservative, and by the turn of the century all senior officers could well remember the masts and yards of the days of sail and the line of battle. Although by 1900 the technological revolution had created new problems for naval tacticians, the big gun still dominated the Royal Navy; and while torpedo-men had attained some slight respectability in forty years, the torpedo and its principal launching platform, the torpedo-boat, were generally associated with weaker navies, such as the French navy, which could no longer hope to challenge Britain in a battle-fleet action.

By the turn of the century the submarine had appeared, the one weapons system the Royal Navy did not need. Many officers recalled the remark of Admiral Earl St Vincent, when Robert Fulton had offered his primitive submarine, *Nautilus*, to a hostile Admiralty in 1804: 'Pitt is the greatest fool that ever existed to encourage a mode of warfare which those who command the seas do not want and, if successful, will deprive them of it.' Britain's command of the seas was assured, they argued, by her battle-fleet and her numerous cruisers. The nation's survival depended on the unhindered maritime trade that brought her the food (in which she was no longer self-sufficient) and the raw materials that would be worked up into finished goods to be exported to pay for her huge imports. The admirals fully understood that, of all countries, Britain was thus the most vulnerable to blockade. Hitherto the mere existence of the British battle-fleet had guaranteed safe passage on the high seas for smaller warships and the merchant shipping of all nations. Now their fear was twofold: that the Royal Navy might not be able to break a submarine blockade, and that the methods of these new blockading vessels would be barbarous. One year after the Royal Navy had acquired its first submarine the much respected Admiral Wilson, then Commander-in-Chief, Channel Fleet, had denounced the underwater weapon as 'underhand, unfair, and damned un-English'. To some officers the submarine captain was no better than a pirate.

The submarine's stealth, her prime attribute, threatened to violate the accepted rules of naval warfare. For a submarine to attack a warship without warning was, of course, a lawful act of war, and no naval officer could seriously complain of that, but to attack a merchant vessel in this way was not permitted. The feeling of outrage at such attacks, sincerely held, was founded upon sound doctrine. A maritime nation dedicated to the idea of free trade and the rights of individuals had a traditional respect for private property. Prince Louis of Battenberg, a future First Sea Lord, had much earlier expressed a typical view: 'The more I think of it, the more difficulty I have in believing that a civilized power would deliberately sanction its armed forces committing wholesale murder on the High Seas.' War might be, and was, conducted between states, but the rules of warfare that had been elaborated over the centuries to impose restraints on belligerents by confining the damage and destruction to public property also provided that the lives and belongings of private individuals should be spared. Thus while a ship under the enemy's national flag might lawfully be taken, this had to be done according to 'prize rules', and these required that the vessel must be ordered to stop by visual signals, a token shot being fired 'across the bow' if necessary. The vessel must be boarded, her papers inspected and the passengers and crew put into a place of safety (if in boats, within easy reach of the shore), or the ship must be sailed into port by a prize crew. Thus, according to the international law of the sea, a submarine on blockade duty was required to operate as a cruiser of the traditional kind, but in acting thus she would forfeit her sole military advantage of stealth. It was generally thought that submarine captains would be obliged to stop and visit and search merchantmen; to sink a vessel without warning would be an act of barbarism which, certainly, no civilized nation would permit. As late as 1912 the Admiralty stated that the submarine had 'the smallest value of any vessel for a direct attack on trade. She does not carry a crew which is capable of taking charge of a prize; she cannot remove passengers and other persons if she wishes to sink one.'

As it happened, the French submarine service achieved little, mainly because France no longer fought her ancient enemy across the Channel, and thus lacked her great opportunity to put to the test the exciting theories of the 'Jeune école', as the aggressive, avant-garde French naval thinkers were called. Surprisingly, in the light of later events, Germany took up the submarine rather late, in 1906, with her first U-boat, *Unter-zeeboot 1*. Germany's naval High Command, like the British Admiralty, did not then see the potential value of the submarine, and Admiral Tirpitz too had begun the construction of a modern navy around a battle-fleet. He and his colleagues had also thought of the submarine as a coast-defence vessel, and they were surprised by the success of their U-boats in the early days of the First World War. A submarine blockade of Britain was instituted in 1915, but U-boat captains, with a few exceptions, genuinely attempted to conduct their commerce raiding according to 'prize rules', often at great risk to themselves. As might have been expected, when the decision to institute unrestricted submarine warfare was taken, the highest interests of the state were urged to excuse this gross breach of long-hallowed international custom. The argument of Germany's Chief of Naval Staff deserves to be quoted at length:

A decision must be reached in the war before the autumn of 1917, if it is not to end in the exhaustion of all parties. . . . If we can break England's back, the war will at once be decided in our favour. . . . the bad harvests in wheat and produce all over the world offer us a quite unique opportunity of which it would be sinful not to take advantage. . . . we can force England to make peace in five months by means of the unrestricted U-boat campaign. . . . in spite of the danger of a break with America, an unrestricted U-boat campaign, begun soon, is the right means to bring the war to a victorious end for us.

Unrestricted submarine warfare involved attack without warning on all ships, Allied or neutral, if they entered a designated zone around the British Isles. The results immediately seemed to justify the German decision, for in one month 354 ships were sunk, a total of more than 800,000 tons, and in 1917 the U-boats sank 2439 ships, totalling 5.5 million tons. This campaign quickly became the gravest threat to the Allied cause. In spite of the mighty and unbeaten Grand Fleet, it seemed that the Royal Navy could do nothing to prevent the daily destruction of ships laden with food and munitions. Jellicoe, by now First Sea Lord, observed, 'It is impossible for us to go on with the war if losses like this continue.' The 'prize rules' drawn up in the days of cruiser warfare, permitting ships to stop, visit, search and sail the prize to port for examination or to ensure the safety of passengers and crew before sinking the vessel, were now ignored. The German submarine service had discovered that the most effective means of waging the war at sea was not by attacking fast, manoeuvrable warships but by indiscriminately sinking isolated merchant vessels without warning. The most successful U-boat tactics were to stalk such ships sailing alone, on the surface, and to destroy them by gunfire so as to conserve the small stock of torpedoes which the U-boats could carry for the most rewarding targets. Her quarry once destroyed, the U-boat would dive to a depth at which she was safe from any chance counter-attack, reappear later and repeat the process.

While Germany's High Seas Fleet was effectively blockaded in harbour by the much stronger Grand Fleet across the North Sea, the U-boats were quietly, efficiently and cheaply achieving what the High Seas Fleet itself had never been expected to do: they were bringing Britain almost to her knees. All her ancient fears were now realized in a quite unexpected way. The privateers had not done as much, and the cruisers and torpedo-boats of unfriendly France could hardly have done more. The distant blockade that the Admiralty had always dreaded was now being enforced by a weapons system to which there was, as yet, no answer. Only the eventual recourse to an ancient remedy, convoy (which is treated in some detail in the next chapter), was to reduce shipping losses to tolerable proportions. It is strange, in retrospect, that the success of this historic policy was even then not widely accepted. Many senior officers appear to have believed that the U-boats had been defeated by the offensive patrols and sweeps made by vastly increased numbers of small ships that had been pressed into service.

After the war feeling against the submarine hardened. Admiral Beatty, now First Sea Lord, himself wrote of the submarine: 'Its use in war tends to outrage the laws of civilization and humanity when in the hands of a weaker power.'

24 The warship that brought Britain close to defeat in two wars: the U-boat. This one was captured. Diesel-electric boats very much like this but larger are still being built.

World opinion was judged to be hostile to any preparations for a repetition of unrestricted submarine warfare, and, certainly, Germany's naval command seemed to have no thought of that; nor did she build any large numbers of U-boats when rearming in the 1930s. More than once in the post-war years the Admiralty seriously proposed the abolition of the submarine as a weapon of war. The new German navy had already begun to take shape as a fairly small and conventional fleet of heavy ships, large armoured cruisers and battleships, with supporting light warships. In 1936 Germany had even subscribed to the London Protocol on Naval Warfare, whereby submarines were to obey 'prize rules', a measure which was expressly intended to make U-boat warfare against merchant shipping impractical. To observe the Protocol a U-boat would have to attack in daylight and on the surface, where she would be a sitting target for an armed merchantman.

There was another, quite different reason why the Admiralty should have some confidence in the outcome of any future U-boat campaign. A highly secret underwater system for detecting submarines, known first as asdic, had been developed by Britain between the wars, and it was believed to be efficient enough to eliminate the submarine menace for good. It is interesting to speculate whether such over-confidence was the unintended by-product of too much secrecy, because there was little practical justification for the Admiralty's faith. Asdic was a remarkable technological breakthrough, based on transmitting through the water, from a dome in the ship's keel, sound waves which were reflected back to an adjacent receiver when they struck a large enough metal object, such as a submarine hull. The natural laws of physics make it very difficult to force sound through water; to do so at any range exceeding a mile or two demands an enormous amount of energy. In its early days this and other problems had not been solved, and by 1939 asdic was not as efficient as many had been led to believe. Moreover, the Royal Navy's small anti-submarine branch was still in embryo; insufficient time was allotted to the training of asdic operators; and anti-submarine exercises were unrealistic. Nor had there been any significant progress in developing better anti-submarine weapons, and the Second World War found destroyers still armed with the First World War depth-charge. A well handled submarine could still escape detection and, if detected, could avoid destruction.

By 1939 the submarine still looked, and in most respects was, much the same boat as the one that had operated to such effect twenty-five years earlier—a diesel-electric submersible with very long range, which could remain submerged, at rest or on passage, for at least twenty-four hours, with a surface speed of 17 knots and able to make about 7 knots when dived. She still had very much the same torpedo, though a form of asdic comparable with that installed in surface ships was just coming into service with the British submarines.

As the Second World War loomed, the U-boat was considered, for many reasons, to be much less of a threat to Allied merchant shipping than the surface raiders, whether the large armoured cruisers or the unknown numbers of auxiliary cruisers converted from merchantmen. As we saw in the previous chapter, the Admiralty had always been obsessed with the threat posed by the surface raider and had made its plans and dispositions accordingly.

In the first phase of the war at sea, between 1939 and 1941, convoy was introduced straightaway in the Western Approaches to the British Isles, but not elsewhere. Germany soon began unrestricted submarine warfare, though the sinking of the passenger liner *Athenia* on the first day of hostilities had been contrary to orders. Admiral Doenitz, the U-boat Commander-in-Chief, deployed no more than fifty-six submarines, fewer than Britain, and less than half this fleet was ocean-going. The U-boats achieved encouraging results in the first year of hostilities. After the fall of France in June 1940, with new submarine bases in western France, they no longer had to transit the Straits of Dover or go north around Scotland to reach the Atlantic, which made gaining their station much less hazardous and their patrols correspondingly more effective.

In October 1940 Doenitz introduced the 'wolfpack' tactic that he had himself conceived in 1917, and by 1941 it was in general use. The 'wolfpack' was a group of as many U-boats as could be quickly gathered in the vicinity of a convoy that was often detected by long-range aircraft and then shadowed by one boat, which had the task of keeping contact and reporting position, course and speed. The U-boats attacked at night, on the surface, not as a torpedo-boat flotilla would but individually, even penetrating the convoy screen so that the primitive radar of the escorting warships could not discriminate between the attackers and their quarry. The U-boat was actually faster on the surface than the Flower-class corvette, which was one of the most numerous type of escort, and because the U-boat was surfaced, the ships' asdic equipment was of no use. The U-boats achieved an early tactical success and a strategic one too. Knowledge of the British naval codes enabled Doenitz to keep an accurate plot of Atlantic convoys, and the advent of larger boats and fuel-tanker submarines enabled more boats to remain longer on station. By 1943 the failure of the small German surface fleet of heavy ships put the U-boat service in the forefront of the German navy, and they were at last given priority in construction. Their campaign reached its peak of success in March 1943, when they were sinking Allied merchant ships faster than they could be built, and more U-boats were going to sea than were being sunk in the great convoy battles. The tide of this second Battle of the Atlantic was turned, and ultimately won, by Allied escort ships and aircraft, using improved radar, night illumination devices and ahead-throwing, ship-mounted anti-submarine weapons—above all, perhaps, by superior Allied intelligence of U-boat movements. Fortunately for the Allies, many sophisticated German technical developments came too late: the acoustic homing torpedo in 1943; the 'schnorkel' breathing tube, which enabled the U-boat to travel underwater, at periscope depth, on her diesel engines in 1944; and the new classes of U-boat which became operational in the last winter of the war, which, if introduced two years sooner, would almost certainly have brought victory to Germany. The U-boat fleet attained its peak strength of 463 boats in March 1945, just two months before the war ended, with new boats that could dive much deeper (600 feet and more, rather than 300 feet) and travel faster underwater (13 knots instead of 7), and not one of their latest boats, the Type XXIII coastal submarine, was lost. The U-boats had come very close to achieving a complete maritime blockade of Britain for the second time in twenty-five years. Their achievement is all the greater in that it was gained by a relatively small section of the German armed forces, one which was not accorded priority of resources until too late. For nearly a century British admirals had been haunted by the spectre of attack on merchant shipping first by cruisers and then by torpedo-boats, but twice in the one generation the threat had been carried to the brink of victory by submarines. Ironically, these near defeats in both battles of the Atlantic were at the hands of a predominantly land power. In the Second World War 1150 U-boats entered service and 632 were sunk at sea, 500 by the Royal Navy and the RAF. For the sacrifice of some 27,000 lives, less than a hundredth part of total German losses, 15 million tons of Allied shipping were lost in nearly 3000 ships.

In one sense, the U-boats were never defeated, for they were still fighting, not without successes, until the very end, when those U-boat captains who were at sea were ordered to surrender, as their predecessors had been in 1918. Their home bases had been overrun, in France in 1944 and in Germany in 1945, and their activities ceased, as they had when the German army had been defeated in the great battles on the Western Front in 1918. It is an interesting paradox that the credit for ending the U-boat menace in 1945 could thus be claimed by the Allied armies; yet these undoubtedly owed their strength to the Allied victory in the Battle of the Atlantic two years earlier.

If the U-boat had brought Germany close to victory, the American submarine service had a large share in the defeat of Japan in a brilliant but largely unknown campaign. Immediately after the Japanese attack on Pearl Harbor that brought the United States into the war, the considerable submarine force of the US Navy began unrestricted warfare in the Pacific. The US Navy had previously allotted the submarine a place in the fleet, as did most navies, but now it quickly saw that if the submarine was the weapon of the weaker naval power, then America had become the weaker naval power in the western Pacific and in the waters around the Japanese islands. With her far-flung garrisons and her dependence on imported fuel and raw materials, Japan resembled Britain: she was vulnerable to blockade.

The Japanese, on the other hand, persisted in employing their submarines as units of the main fleet, and Japanese submarine commanders were trained to believe it more fitting to attack warships, so they never seriously menaced shipping off the West Coast of the United States, as the U-boats did off the Eastern seaboard and in the Caribbean. In contrast, the Americans adopted a bold strategy, overcame the chief difficulty, which was to find reliable torpedoes, and accounted for more than half of the 8 million tons of Japanese merchant shipping lost (nearly the entire mercantile marine) and 200 warships, at the price of some fifty American submarines. By this blockade alone Japan's war industry was brought almost to a halt.

That the British submarine service achieved more modest results compared with the success of the German and American submarine fleets was not because its captains and crews lacked

skill or courage or even first-rate equipment, but because a continental power such as Germany presented fewer targets—though
there were to be plenty of opportunities to demonstrate the
bravery of British submarine crews. Germany's merchant
marine was relatively small; British cruisers, as in the First
World War, maintained a reasonably effective distant blockade
of the German coastline and the coast of occupied Europe.
German shipping sailed along that coastline and in the Baltic
Sea, while during the North African campaign German and
Italian convoys ran across the narrows from Italy with
reinforcements and resupply for their armies. In all these waters
the submarine is bound to operate under the disadvantages of
short routes, plentiful air and surface escorts and usually shallow
water (with the additional hazard of minefields); all of these
factors contributed to the loss of eighty-two British submarines,
of which forty-six were sunk in the Mediterranean. Against the
odds, their deeds must be considered heroic, and by the
combined efforts of the submarine service, maritime aircraft and
surface warships General Rommel's army was eventually denied
the munitions and fuel it required for further offensives in the
desert. In the war against Japan British submarine captains were
to repeat the exploits of their predecessors in the First World
War—not in the Baltic or the Sea of Marmara, as before, but in
the waters around Indonesia and Malaya—often choosing the
gun rather than the torpedo against the small vessels they mostly
encountered.

A new dimension opened with the successful development,
after many years of experiment, of the midget submarine, which
deserves a short digression from the main submarine story.
Although the history of the submarine abounds with examples of
captains taking their boats inside ports and harbours believed to
be impregnable (as when Lieutenant Prien took his U-boat
inside the defences of Scapa Flow to torpedo the battleship
Royal Oak in 1939), even bolder strokes were achieved with
midget craft, such as the Italian navy attack on the British battle-
fleet in Alexandria with 'chariots'. The chariot was essentially no
more than a torpedo with its own intrepid rider who sat on top to
steer it and to affix its warhead to the bottom of the target ship.
The battleships *Queen Elizabeth* and *Valiant* were thus disabled
for many months, though the success of the attack was kept
secret. The Japanese also employed midget submarines, first at
Pearl Harbor and later in Sydney Harbour, but with negligible

results. The German midget submarines which were sent against the Normandy invasion fleets and, later, against Allied shipping bound for Antwerp likewise achieved little.

The British use of the midget submarine was on a smaller scale than that of the German navy, but some notable successes were gained. A few X-craft, as they were called, towed to Norway by conventional submarines, managed to penetrate undetected into the narrow fjord where the battleship *Tirpitz* lay. At least two of the X-craft succeeded in placing and detonating their huge charges beneath the battleship and put her out of the war for many months. By this daring attack the Royal Navy was relieved of its great anxiety that this very powerful ship might break out to menace the Allied convoys to the Soviet Union and in the Atlantic. Near the war's end similar X-craft successfully attacked a Japanese heavy cruiser at Singapore and cut the undersea cable communications between Japan, Hong Kong and Saigon.

By the end of the Second World War the submarine had proved herself a deadly and yet economical weapon. Essentially, however, she was the same vessel as those first experimental boats of nearly half a century before. During the next ten or fifteen years many improvements were made in speed, greater diving depth, the breathing tube, radar, sonar (as asdic was now called), communications, homing torpedoes and the like. The diesel-electric boat, thus brought up to date, remained the mainstay of the world's submarine fleets until the mid-1950s, when the first nuclear-powered submarine emerged—the true submarine at last. All earlier submarines had been in practice no more than submersible torpedo-boats and, indeed, were so employed for much of their time. The nuclear-powered boat herself has effectively unlimited endurance; she is restricted only by that of her crew. Her nuclear power plant can recycle the air in the boat, so she needs no breathing tube, and it purifies sea water for drinking. She does not need to cruise at periscope depth, nor does she transit on the surface, as earlier submarines commonly did. She can proceed underwater at 30 knots or more, and she can dive to vastly greater depths than her predecessors. The nature of her power plant, the nuclear reactor, dictates her size—at least three times greater than that of a diesel-electric boat, in some cases ten times larger. As big as a cruiser, she roams the deep sea almost invulnerable. She is, perhaps, the capital ship of the navy.

From the first, two distinct types of nuclear-powered submarine were built, the ballistic missile-firing submarine (SSBN), whose development is separate from the mainstream of the submarine story, and the attack or hunter-killer submarine (SSN), whose principal task is to find and destroy other submarines, including the SSBN. The strategic deterrent under the sea, carried in a vessel dedicated to that purpose and to no other, has something in common with the battle-fleet of old.

25 The strategic nuclear deterrent: a Soviet ballistic missile-firing submarine of the Delta class.

Indeed, the Strategic Arms Limitation Talks between the super-powers today have the same objectives as did the Naval Conferences fifty years ago, when the then super-powers agreed on limits to battleship numbers and size. Before, during and after the First World War there was no more important task for the British battle-fleet than simply to exist and, by existing, to deter maritime threats from any other power. To an even greater extent today, it is the presence on station of the SSBNs of the four powers which deploy them, rather than their actual power to win a battle or a war, that acts as a deterrent. Such boats (and they are still called boats, even at their present size of 18,000 tons) are manned and operated by navies for obvious reasons, but they live apart from the rest of each navy. In the great oceans which cover three-quarters of the surface of the world such submarines are virtually undetectable, though they can be heard on passage at speed by passive sonars emplaced on the sea bed. These considerations apply, in some respects only, to the SSN, but her purpose, and therefore her operational profile, are entirely different and her chance of detection correspondingly somewhat higher.

The extraordinary advance, in every respect by which the power of a submarine may be measured and compared, which has flowed from the qualities of the nuclear-powered attack submarine discussed above might be supposed to have rendered all diesel-electric submersibles obsolete overnight, rather as *Dreadnought* superseded earlier battleships fifty years ago. This has not happened for three quite separate reasons, economic, industrial and military. These can be briefly stated. A nuclear-powered attack submarine costs between three and four times as much as a conventional boat (SSK), takes about twice as long to build and is at a disadvantage in shallow or narrow waters because she is so much bigger. These highly practical arguments have ensured the continued building and vigorous technical development of diesel-electric submersibles in those navies which are able to build both. It is for these reasons that the Royal Navy has just embarked on the design of a new conventional boat after a gap of some ten years or more. There are, of course, many navies in the world which do not have the choice, lacking the nuclear expertise to build reactors at all, let alone to cope with the infinitely more difficult task of designing and installing a version which will operate safely and surely in a submarine.

Submarine warfare will undoubtedly continue as long as maritime war itself does, and there can be no doubt that the advent of nuclear power in these boats and the dramatic advances in the weapons that all submarines now deploy will make it an even more desperate and dangerous game. The classic duel between new weapons and the defence against them, like that fought years ago between shell and armour, is now being vigorously pursued in the research laboratories as well as in the naval staff headquarters of all the maritime powers.

The submarine can now carry guided and homing missiles which are fired submerged against other submarines and out to ranges of 200 or 300 miles against surface ships, with most of their trajectory in air. These new boats have active and passive sensors not only to locate their targets but also to warn them if they are themselves being stalked. Coupled with their high submerged speed and ability to go very deep, this makes them hard to locate, difficult to catch and awkward to destroy. No single weapons platform will now succeed against them, and their destruction has become very much a team operation, of which the co-operation between surface escorts and maritime aircraft at the close of the Second World War must be regarded as the beginning, although the team must now be bigger and better equipped. The helicopter has proved an excellent anti-submarine weapons system and is now embarked in that role in all modern escorts. Detection capability has greatly improved, though there is no sign of a technical breakthrough which can overcome the physical difficulty of forcing sound waves through sea water. Long-range maritime aircraft with much more efficient sensors and weapons are now an integral part of all anti-submarine operations, and the nuclear-powered attack sub-marine is regarded by many as the strongest member of this large and diverse team. The weapons available to the team are at the frontiers of technology and include highly sophisticated guided and homing missiles (still, rather strangely, called torpedoes), long-range air-flight weapons, which enter the water close to the submarine target and home on to it, and even nuclear depth bombs.

Submariners claim that naval warfare is dominated by the submarine, even more than it was in the two great wars of this century. In both the submarine proved herself the most dangerous threat to maritime nations dependent on the movement of merchant shipping both for their survival and for their capacity to further the maritime strategy of carrying the war to the enemy's continental landmass. The submarine was then the secondary weapon of a continental power, Germany, and very nearly proved more than equal to the primary weapon, the surface fleet, of the major maritime power, Britain. Today another predominantly continental power, the Soviet Union, has 300 attack submarines (ninety of them nuclear-powered), compared with the fifty-odd with which Doenitz started his war in 1939. Against them are ranged the anti-submarine forces of the NATO Alliance, much smaller now in numbers than those of the Royal Navy and the RAF which managed to hold

on alone, and by the skin of their teeth, from 1939 to 1942.

By way of a tailpiece to the submarine story, we may mention that there are those who envisage a time when all warships will go under water, leaving the surface apparently empty except for the world's merchant marine. But, immensely powerful as the modern submarine is, she can project power (or political influence) only by actually fighting, for there are no rungs on the ladder of escalation of underwater conflict. Surface ships, by contrast, are suited to a wide range of naval and constabulary action falling well short of actual hostilities. Moreover, a surface fleet is highly visible, and it may well be that it is precisely that visibility, just as much as the invisible presence of the ballistic

26 Two ways of destroying enemy submarines. The nuclear-powered 'fleet', 'attack' or 'hunter-killer' submarine and the Sea King anti-submarine helicopter, of the type embarked in the Invincible class.

missile submarines, that will keep the peace. SSBNs may well be today's battle-fleet, the ultimate deterrent, but they can threaten only Armageddon, nothing less. They, or any other submarines on the surface, are really fish out of water; as militarily insignificant as a surface ship under the sea.

Chapter 8
DESTROYER

> ... *we find ourselves involved in an effort to restore to the flotilla some of its old cruiser capacity, by endowing it with gun armament, higher sea-keeping power, and facilities for distant communication, all at the cost of specialization and of greater economic strain ... no point has been found at which it was possible to stop the tendency of this class of vessel to increase in size and cost. ...*
>
> SIR JULIAN CORBETT, *Some Principles of Maritime Strategy*, 1911

> ... *we planned our fleet with too little emphasis on the escort-of-convoy function. On the other hand, the fleet destroyer flotillas of 1939 ... were the cream of the Royal Navy.*
>
> CAPTAIN STEPHEN ROSKILL, *The War at Sea*, 1961

On 15 June 1942 Captain C. C. Hardy, Royal Navy, in the old anti-aircraft cruiser *Cairo*, with five fleet destroyers and four escort destroyers, was escorting a convoy through the narrows to Malta when an enemy force of two cruisers and five destroyers was reported. Hardy's fleet destroyers promptly attacked, although they were outranged by the cruisers' heavier guns. Two British destroyers were soon disabled, but the other three pressed home their attack. The senior destroyer officer, Commander B. G. Scurfield, afterwards wrote: 'This is what I had been training for, for twenty-two years, and I led my five destroyers up towards the enemy. I was in a fortunate position in many ways, and I knew what we had to do. The cost was not to be counted. The ship was as ready for the test as we had been able to make her. I could do no more about it.'

The destroyer, or torpedo-boat destroyer, which emerged in the 1890s as part of a second revolution in the technology of naval warfare, joined the battleship and the cruiser. During the previous thirty years the world's navies had completed the first revolution made possible by developments in heavy industry.

27 Cheap and fast, the early torpedo-boat proved too small for any but a calm sea and was less successful than the submarine and the aircraft, yet she began a counter-revolution in naval warfare.

The wooden-walled sailing ships, with muzzle-loading cannon firing solid shot, had given way to steamships with bigger guns firing armour-piercing shell, which greatly extended the range at which sea battles could be fought. From the 1820s the gradual introduction of the steam engine enabled gunboats, cruisers and line-of-battle ships to proceed independently of the wind, while first iron and then steel made them stronger armoured ships. All these changes, which came about in the latter half of the nineteenth century, increased the offensive power of the world's navies to an extent unimaginable fifty years earlier. The new steam gunboats, iron-hulled, were now able to open up Africa and China, but the line-of-battle ship did not change her function when she came to be called 'battleship' in the 1880s, and the steel-hulled cruiser was still expected to enforce the close blockade of the previous century, very much in the manner of her predecessors under sail. A revolution had taken place at sea, but the counter-revolution came almost at once. This is the history of warfare.

Whitehead's torpedo appeared in 1866, just six years after the world's first ironclad. The mine, known at first as a torpedo, already existed and was moored in fairly shallow water to explode on contact with a ship's hull. It could also be remotely detonated from the shore by electricity. Such mines were passive and immobile and were soon developed into the much more dangerous 'locomotive' mine, to be known henceforth as the *torpedo*. The moored mine was simple and cheap, the torpedo complicated and expensive, but one mine or torpedo, holing a ship under the waterline, could do more damage than many armour-piercing shells striking the deck and sides of an ironclad. The mine and the torpedo forced those much more powerful and essentially offensive weapons systems, the battleship, the cruiser and the gunboat, on to the defensive. Henceforth the battleship could put to sea with safety only when screened by a flotilla of escort vessels and preceded by mine-sweeping craft if near the coast, while fleet anchorages or lesser harbours and ports required elaborate defences, including huge wire nets to enclose big ships at anchor. The cruiser was obliged to abandon her traditional war station near the enemy coast, and close blockade had to give way to distant blockade, while the gunboat vanished from European waters. All this was to be achieved not by building a rival to the world's largest battle-fleet or a host of cruisers, but by providing the torpedo with a cheap 'launching platform'.

The early torpedo had a very short range, only a few hundred yards, so it had to be brought close to its target and launched from a favourable position. The little torpedo-boat, only 90 feet long, appeared to be the answer to the naval supremacy of the hitherto unchallenged battle-fleet. Soon France was said to have eighty first-class sea-going torpedo-boats in the English Channel, although in any sea the craft were slow and very wet. The response to the torpedo-boat was defensive gunfire. Battleships were fitted with light, quick-firing guns, even machine-guns. The torpedo-gunboat, hurriedly introduced to catch the 20-knot torpedo-boat, proved too slow, and by the early 1890s the torpedo-boat destroyer appeared, twice as large as the torpedo-boat and much faster—27 knots at first, 36 knots by 1907. Because of her size, the torpedo-boat destroyer was a better sea-boat and mounted torpedo tubes as well as quick-firing guns. Thus the destroyer (the name to which the earlier designation was quickly shortened) was herself a more reliable torpedo-boat, able to keep up with the battle-fleet in all but heavy seas, to steam at high speed to intercept enemy torpedo-boats (or enemy torpedo-boat destroyers) and to attack the enemy battle-fleet with torpedoes. The fleet destroyer had joined the cruisers and the battleships. As escort and screen, she was much smaller than the light cruiser but faster and handier, with a smaller crew and cheaper. The destroyer quickly became a general-purpose vessel, like the sloop, but with a far more damaging punch, both in guns and torpedoes. She could scout ahead and run errands for the Commander-in-Chief; as a back-up to the fleet mine-sweeper which was specially designed and therefore better suited to this task, she could also, by 1915, stream wire sweeps ahead of the battle-fleet to cut moored mines adrift. Fast, heavily armed (but never armoured), the fleet destroyer was handsome, glamorous and fashionable. British destroyer captains were brilliant ship handlers and gallant fighters, even if, in the early years, they were often lacking in technical knowledge—in Churchill's words, they were 'more captains of ships than captains of war'.

28 'Light cavalry', 1914: torpedo-boat destroyers at sea.

The tiny first-generation torpedo-boats disappeared fast once the torpedo-boat destroyer made her entry on the naval scene, and her adversary became a torpedo craft more her own size — 300 tons and upwards, the British 'M' class of 1914–17 being of 1200 tons. Although in the early 1900s destroyer flotillas had been assigned a secondary torpedo attack role, by 1914 the British destroyer was primarily a gun platform, with a heavier armament than the corresponding German craft and mounting fewer torpedo tubes. By the time of Jutland a destroyer attack on the battle-fleet was a hazardous and uncertain business because the effective range of the torpedo was much less than 5 miles. To press home their attack so close in daylight (or when illuminated by searchlights at night), the flotillas were obliged to sail well inside the range of the battleship's secondary armament of 6-inch guns, and few got through. At Jutland one old German battleship (the only one lost that day) was sunk by torpedoes from a destroyer, and in that great action destroyers fought destroyers.

29 The fleet destroyer (1939–45), still fast and glamorous. Fleet destroyer tactics scarcely changed in two world wars.

Between the wars the large, fast, heavily armed fleet destroyer became an essential unit of all ocean-going navies. The French and Italians built big, very fast ships for the Mediterranean, but they were comparatively short-range vessels, not designed for Atlantic conditions. Japanese destroyers were also fast and heavily armed with both guns and torpedo tubes, and the US Navy settled on building a most successful standard type, which served throughout the Second World War. The Royal Navy came late to the very large, powerful destroyer with the famous Tribal class, and other excellent designs followed.

But between the wars, as we have noted in earlier chapters, naval thinking continued, in spite of the evidence of the first Battle of the Atlantic, to hark back to the battle-fleet, to the worldwide deployment of cruisers for both the protection and the destruction of sea-borne commerce and a slowly growing emphasis on maritime air operations with the advance of aircraft-carriers and the parallel advance of aircraft suitable for operation from their decks. As we have also pointed out, a subject to which minimal attention was devoted was that of convoy. The large and diverse organization and the many ships with a mainly anti-submarine role which were required to implement this (certainly, to the British) vital form of defence, were largely neglected. Convoy escorts were no good to the battle-fleet. They had no offensive capability. They were small, dull ships, and Naval Staffs were understandably reluctant to devote hard-won resources to them when it seemed that the money would be better spent on the big ships and their traditional offensive and defensive support. The question of whether or not, in the circumstances, this was an error of judgement must remain highly controversial. What can scarcely be denied is that the blind spot was to cost Britain dear—it nearly cost her the war that was about to come.

The whole question of convoy deserves a closer look here, not only because it merits discussion in its own right but also because it will help us to locate the broad destroyer concept accurately in the grave events which were to ensue in the second Battle of the Atlantic. The necessarily brief examination of the convoy story which follows illuminates the part which the big fleet destroyer was required to play in it, and why the destroyer was found less than satisfactory in this role, for which she had not been designed. The very different type of escort which was developed to do the job emerges, and finally we may trace the clear effect which all these dramatic events had on the evolution of the destroyer of the 1980s. Whether she is now called destroyer or frigate, sloop or escort, her lineage is clear, even if it has taken thirty years of argument and uncertainty for her to assume her present powerful but extremely costly form.

The starting point must be the arrival on the naval scene of the torpedo-boat and its instant threat to what may be regarded as a very special sort of convoy, the battle-fleet. Although the torpedo-boat was fairly quickly supplanted by the destroyer herself, new kinds of torpedo-launching platform emerged, and for a time each would force the destroyer back on to the defensive. The high-speed (35–45 knot) coastal motor-boat, mounting two or four torpedo tubes, offered a smaller and faster target than the original torpedo-boat, and in 1918 such craft sank a battleship of the Austro-Hungarian navy in the Adriatic, but they were limited to narrow coastal waters. They could best be met by destroyer gunfire and also by high-speed craft of their own kind, mounting more machine-guns, especially 20-mm cannon, and eventually medium-calibre guns up to a battleship's secondary armament. The air-launched torpedo was more dangerous, even to fast warships at sea with room to manoeuvre and a clear field of fire, and infinitely more to the slow, unarmed merchant ship. The 'torpedo-aircraft destroyer' (to coin an ugly term) assumed more than one form. It could even be another aircraft of the fast interceptor-fighter type, or it could be a destroyer-type vessel mounting dual-purpose quick-firing guns which could also destroy the high-speed motor-torpedo-boat. Thus by the Second World War a specialist destroyer was beginning to appear to protect coastal shipping from air and surface torpedo attack and from air bombing. The British Hunt class (1940–2) were of this type, while some of the older fleet destroyers were adapted for the purpose, losing torpedo tubes in exchange for additional quick-firing guns.

An even greater menace than the aircraft was the submarine, in this context a submersible torpedo-boat. The submarine would certainly be vulnerable to destroyer gunfire while she remained on the surface, but once submerged, there was for twenty years no way of locating her. A First World War device, the hydrophone, merely picked up the noise of a submarine's propeller but gave no indication of direction or range. Asdic, the underwater echo-ranging system that was urgently developed between the wars and has been known since the Second World

War by its American name, sonar, was very far from having been perfected by 1939. The search for an underwater detection device took some strange forms. It was found that a pair of sea-lions borrowed from a zoo responded to the noise of a submarine's propeller. The experiments were first conducted in a swimming pool, where the animals were rewarded with fish. Later sea trials proved disappointing, however, because the creatures either could not or would not distinguish between the noise of a submarine and any other craft, and in the open sea they preferred to catch their own fish! This experiment should not be dismissed as too fanciful, for research continues today on the same lines with dolphins, and some remarkably successful results have been obtained.

The only weapon that could be used against a suspected submarine was an explosive charge dropped over the side or stern above the estimated position of the enemy. This depth-charge, a large cylindrical drum containing 250 pounds of explosive, was pre-set to detonate at the supposed depth of the submarine, but only by great good luck would it explode close enough to damage the submarine's pressure-hull, and if the attacking ship failed to clear the area quickly enough, she could well blow her own propellers off.

Such was the state of the defence when Germany began unrestricted submarine warfare in 1917, and it had not changed very much by 1939. The mine and the torpedo had curbed the offensive power of those traditional enforcers of blockade, the cruisers, backed by the battle-fleet, but the torpedo (and, in a quite different way, the mine) was to become more than merely a defensive weapon, for in the hands of a weaker naval power it developed into the most effective means of counter-blockade, and the greater threat was to the merchant marine of a maritime nation such as Britain. As targets for the torpedo, warships are fast and manoeuvrable, designed to withstand damage and well armed, while merchant vessels are slower, unwieldy, generally less well protected and, even in time of war, less well armed or not armed at all, unlike the powerful East Indiamen of two centuries ago. Britain's huge merchant fleet had always been vulnerable to attack. In the Napoleonic Wars commerce raiding by marauding cruisers and by smaller craft in the Channel had been a menace, even after the victory at Trafalgar. During the intervening century or so of peace the Admiralty had watched uneasily the building of French or American or Russian cruisers which could destroy British trade; in the twentieth century the submarine emerged as a rival to the cruiser. Yet when unrestricted submarine warfare was adopted in 1917 and effectively a German counter-blockade of Britain was instituted, the Royal Navy was singularly ill-prepared for it.

In the third month of unrestricted submarine war the U-boats sank 354 merchantmen, of 800,000 tons. The world's greatest battle-fleet had been victorious at Jutland—in so far as it had kept the German battle-fleet in harbour—but it proved powerless to save the merchant marine. Defeat stared the Allies in the face. The Admiralty had no solution, except for advising ships' masters about the route to sail. Those merchantmen that were armed were torpedoed without warning instead of being sunk more cheaply by gunfire from a surfaced U-boat. A vast flotilla of light craft, from destroyers to motor launches, was engaged in continuous offensive patrolling and in 'sweeps', but to no avail. The sinkings continued.

There was a solution, and indeed it had been selectively adopted at the start of hostilities in 1914, mainly for fast liners carrying troops in convoy. We may here define this historically well tried defensive formation as an organized group of ships escorted by men-of-war (and later by aircraft as well). For a long time, however, the Admiralty was reluctant to adopt convoy as a comprehensive measure. The official view was expressed that the convoy provided an ideal target for submarines, that each convoy would need a huge escort, that so many ships cleared British ports every week that convoy was impracticable. The Admiralty argued that convoys could not be assembled in neutral ports, that ships would be held up for weeks, that congestion in home ports would cause further delays, that the consequent loss of shipping space would be unacceptable. It maintained that a convoy stood in greater danger than would the individual ships sailing by themselves, and that the larger the convoy the greater the danger.

In all these respects the Admiralty was proved wrong. Steamships could keep station in convoy; ships in convoy were safer than individually routed ships; the larger the convoy the safer it was and, proportionately, the fewer were the escorts required to screen its perimeter. Sensible organization ensured that the arrival and departure of convoys did not cause congestion in the ports. The Admiralty had misread the shipping statistics, which included data for small coasters and ferries, to arrive at a figure of thousands of ships entering and leaving port every week, whereas only two or three hundred of these were ocean-going vessels. The truth may well have been that the Admiralty disliked convoy because it was a defensive strategy, and naval officers believed in the offensive. They had been taught that their aim must be the destruction of the enemy's forces. While often sound enough in land warfare, the same considerations did not apply to the sea. The destruction of the enemy's fleet in battle was desirable, but it was not essential. Sea power could thus avert defeat by blockade and assure victory on land—navies can lose wars, but they cannot win them. Such, indeed, was to be the maritime strategy adopted by Britain in the two great wars of the twentieth century, but in 1917 this was hard for some naval officers to understand. Schooled in the doctrine of the offensive, they thought the war at sea could be won by victory over the High Seas Fleet. That victory had been duly won the year before at Jutland, in spite of the failure to destroy that fleet, but the U-boat menace remained.

Hundreds of flotilla vessels were now to be employed in patrols and sweeps to clear the trade routes of enemy submarines. By contrast, the routine of convoy escort was seen as passive and perhaps as unworthy of the heirs to the tradition of Rodney and Nelson—although their illustrious predecessors had always seen convoy as an important and successful part of their strategy. While offensive patrols and sweeps continued, the Admiralty considered offensive action against the U-boats in their bases. The strategy was sound enough, and indeed it proved successful when the German armies were defeated in the field in 1918 and again in 1945. But to seize and hold heavily defended naval bases in Germany itself or German-occupied territory in the midst of the war was not feasible unless the entire German front collapsed. However, until the idea of close blockade was abandoned shortly before 1914, the Admiralty had argued in favour of attacks on German naval bases such as Wilhelmshaven, although the General Staff had been quite opposed to such a concept. The daunting success of the U-boat offensive prompted the Admiralty to try again by requesting a large-scale army offensive in Belgium in order to capture the submarine bases on the Flanders coast, although these were known to be by no means the most important ones. The resulting third battle of Ypres, in the autumn of 1917, was costly in human life but brought the army no nearer to the U-boats, while in the following year an amphibious raid, carried out with great gallantry, failed to block the Flanders bases.

The increasingly bleak record of sinkings in this first Battle of the Atlantic and the failure of the offensive sea patrols as well as the land campaigns drove the Admiralty reluctantly to adopt a comprehensive convoy system. It was an immediate success. Where in the days of individual sailings a U-boat captain might have expected to find one merchantman after another, he now had only a fleeting opportunity to sight a convoy, and when it came within torpedo range he could attack only once before having to position his boat afresh for another attack. This could be done in time only by moving at top speed on the surface, under the guns of the convoy's escorting warships, and the U-boat would be under attack from the moment her presence was known. Her captain was less likely to find a convoy, and if he did, the convoy's escorts were very much more likely to catch him there than if they patrolled wide stretches of ocean. So it is no surprise that after the general adoption of convoy more U-boats were to be sunk by the escorts than by offensive patrols and hunting groups. All the same, the Admiralty insisted that convoy was merely a palliative measure and not a substitute for seeking out and destroying the U-boats; in the belief that the best form of defence was attack, it persisted with 'hunting groups', with little success. This policy is an excellent example of the consequences of forgetting or misapplying the first lesson at all staff colleges, which is to select the aim—and the proper aim then was (and still is) the safe and timely arrival of the convoy. As an historian of the time has put it, sinking submarines was 'a bonus, not a necessity'.

As we mentioned in chapter seven, unreasonable confidence in the efficacy of asdic had, by the late 1930s, led the Admiralty to believe that a destroyer so fitted could certainly detect and destroy any submarine, and thus it did not expect a renewal of unrestricted submarine warfare. It was thought that in a future war ships might well have to be sailed in convoy, but there was little high-level interest in convoy defence, and most exercises between the wars involved the interception of a surface raider by British cruisers, not the defence of a North Atlantic convoy against attack by U-boats and aircraft. In all fairness to the Admiralty, it must be remembered that until Germany presented an obvious threat to world peace from 1935 onwards, war was expected to be with Japan. The Royal Navy, accordingly, had to be prepared for a battle-fleet action in the south-west Pacific or the Indian Ocean rather than the North Atlantic, and when it seemed probable that the Royal Navy would have to fight Germany and Italy as well as Japan, it was by no means certain that the principal threat would come from the U-boat. All three likely opponents were building fast battleships and heavy cruisers. There was no evidence that the German navy contemplated another U-boat campaign, and there was strong evidence that the German naval staff itself did not. Germany had even subscribed to the international Protocol of 1936, outlawing unrestricted submarine warfare against merchant shipping, and at the start of the Second World War German U-boat strength was only fifty-six, of which but two dozen boats were ocean-going. However soundly based this inter-war judgement may have been, the second Battle of the Atlantic was joined with a vengeance almost as soon as the Second World War began, and it was to last throughout the entire European war, nearly six long years. It was a battle lost and won several times. Until quite late on it was fought with weapons not greatly different from those used in the previous conflict, and many of the destroyers were themselves veterans of 1918.

The term 'destroyer' is used here (and for the first time) to describe all escort vessels of about destroyer size and of a defensive type—sloop, corvette, frigate, as well as the fleet destroyer converted to anti-submarine work and the much later escort destroyer especially designed for convoy duties. Frigates were once sailing vessels doing the work of cruisers, and a century and half later steam-driven frigates entered the Battle of the Atlantic. They were larger and faster than the little corvettes (the French name for sloops), small, general-purpose warships or gunboats. At the onset of war the burden was borne by the old destroyers, soon to be followed by the famous Flower-class corvettes, of which nearly 300 were built for the British and Canadian navies. Designed originally for coastal waters, they were really too small for the North Atlantic, though that is where most of them were to serve so well.

The principal weapon then available to all these escorts was still (as in 1917 and 1918) the depth-charge, thrown abeam or rolled over the stern of the destroyer or dropped from aircraft. Much later in the war the Hedgehog mortar appeared, an ahead-throwing device firing twenty-four small bombs, any of which would explode on contact with the submarine. This was followed by the Squid, which fired three large depth-charges. Ahead-throwing weapons enabled the destroyer to maintain asdic contact with the target until the last moment and thus to reduce the time available for the submarine to take avoiding action. Refinements in depth-charge tactics included the 'creep attack', a very thorough operation in which one ship kept asdic contact, directing her consort to release a large number of depth-charges at the right point. Such deliberate attacks required an additional 'hunter-killer' group of destroyers, which could hold the U-boat contact while the convoy escort sailed clear, but there was always a dearth of ships for convoy duty. A deep-dived U-boat could usually avoid detection and might escape unless the destroyers could afford to wait for thirty-six hours or so, when the U-boat captain would be compelled to surface for air to breathe and to recharge his batteries.

30 Both the little corvette (1940) and those who sailed in her were 'for hostilities only'.

The best position for a U-boat captain to fire torpedoes from was ahead of the convoy, on either bow, so the convoy was disposed with ships in line abreast, in several short columns to reduce the chance of a hit. Forty ships would form four-deep in ten columns, the convoy commodore (usually a senior retired naval officer) leading in the centre column and the escort group commander in one of the half-dozen or so destroyers of the close escort, his ships' asdics sweeping 70 degrees on either bow. The formation was thus 8 or 10 miles wide and not quite as deep; the thirty-ship convoys of 1942 grew to twice as many vessels a year or two later. The escorts' chief task was to detect and attack a submerged U-boat before she got into position to fire her torpedoes at about 3000 yards' range. In darkness a surfaced U-boat might be detected a little further away, but the fairly primitive radar of the early war years would not always pick up her small profile, and in such an attack a boat on the surface could not be detected by asdic. A slow convoy made an average speed of only 7 knots, and most of the so-called fast convoys barely 3 knots more. It was easy for a 'wolfpack' of U-boats to trail a convoy, working by night, cruising on the surface like torpedo-boats, trying to get inside the convoy's protective screen, and in this mode a U-boat could actually travel faster than a corvette.

Britain was desperately short of suitable convoy escorts when the second Battle of the Atlantic began, so the magnificent force of fleet destroyers, fast and heavily armed (and designed for offensive protection of the battle-fleet), had to be thrown at once into this very different battle, with grievous losses in the first two years. In many respects they were unsuitable for the task: they were over-armed and lacked the specialized anti-submarine weapons that were needed. Moreover, they did not have the endurance to stay with the convoy for a couple of weeks rather than days, often steaming fast to find and kill their new enemy under, rather than on, the surface. While the older fleet destroyers of First World War design and construction could be and were adapted for long Atlantic passages, in developing the latest large, powerful fleet destroyers British naval architects had not been asked to design a ship large enough to provide a reasonably dry, stable platform in the kind of sea peculiar to the Atlantic. Even the wartime Hunt-class escort destroyers were not a complete success in the narrow seas for which they were intended, not least because they lacked endurance. Convoy escort meant ceaseless vigil round the clock. The relentless note of the asdic 'pinging' ahead day and night kept those on the tiny open bridge of the escort destroyer waiting for the echo that indicated a possible submarine. The captain seldom hesitated to attack at once, with depth-charges set to 150 feet; then he waited until the turbulent water had settled before beginning a deliberate search, but often there was nothing to hunt.

As the war progressed, the long-range aircraft proved to be a most effective destroyer of U-boats. Strategically, aircraft could reach the battleground within hours of a sighting report. Tactically, an aircraft could search by day and night with radar, approaching a surfaced U-boat rapidly, dropping depth-charges before she had time to dive deep. Like the warships, the aircraft found more targets by shadowing a convoy than by routine patrolling, although U-boats returning to their base in France were vulnerable in the Bay of Biscay. There were not enough long-range aircraft for the first three years of the Second World War; service in Coastal Command of the RAF did not have the glamour and excitement of Bomber or Fighter Command; and the best machines were not always provided. Although Coastal Command eventually came under the operational control of the Admiralty, it was a long time before the Command had enough strike aircraft and long-range fighters for maritime work. Before the battle was won Coastal Command had become a powerful and highly efficient member of the team, yet it must be said that the lack of a balanced maritime air component of the Royal Navy was, from the onset, a serious handicap to Britain. The Royal Navy's relatively few ship-borne aircraft did, of course, make an important contribution to the victory; in the end they and the long-range bomber aircraft destroyed as many U-boats at sea as did the destroyers and other escort vessels. Despite some success against U-boats on passage from their bases, most of the 'kills' were made in the one place where the U-boat had to disclose her presence, near a convoy. In this respect the future of anti-submarine warfare might be seen already, since it soon became a team effort involving surface ships, aircraft, and even our own submarines.

The Battle of the Atlantic was the Royal Navy's greatest campaign in both wars. It was as if the navy had to fight a fleet action of Jutland proportions every day of the week for several years. In both conflicts, and certainly in the Second World War, most, if not all, the conventional naval battles involving British warships and most dispositions of the fleets were contingent upon, and related to, the movement of British shipping. Thus in 1941 the Home Fleet fought *Bismarck*, and two years later *Scharnhorst*, to protect the convoys of merchantmen. The same Home Fleet was constantly sailed in support to provide cover for the Atlantic and Russian convoys. Battleships and cruisers defended convoys with gunfire; and the destroyers' defence trade was not confined to repelling U-boats or aircraft. Captain Sherbrooke's gallant shielding of the Russia-bound convoy JW 51B, pitting his destroyers against a German heavy squadron until the cruisers *Jamaica* and *Sheffield* came to the rescue, Commander Scurfield's brave defence of a convoy attacked by a superior Italian force, and Captains Micklethwait's and Poland's repeated engagement of a greatly superior enemy force, which included a battleship, in defence of a Malta-bound convoy, are among the more notable examples of the fleet destroyer fighting defensively, as she was designed to do, against other ships with gun, torpedo and smoke rather than with the depth-charge.

The defensive was not merely the prelude to an eventual offensive strategy in which armies would be ferried to the enemy's mainland. Those armies had to be maintained, supported, reinforced, and thus the maritime allied nations, Britain and the United States, remained on the defensive. Naval warfare was not—and never had been—an end in itself. It was, rather, a means to an end: the protection of one's own shipping and the destruction or immobilization of enemy shipping. In this strategy 'command of the sea' meant not the guarding of large areas of ocean, but the protection of ships, and history has shown that the best way of doing that is through the introduction of convoy.

The widespread and increasing use of ever more sophisticated mines, though not part of the convoy story (except, perhaps, at second remove), greatly complicated the task of protecting British (and later Allied) shipping and added another to the long list of tasks for which the destroyer became the first line of defence. Throughout the Second World War Britain's coastal traffic was at risk, but with the reopening of the Western Front in 1944 and the clearance of the sea approach to the great port of Antwerp, a mere couple of dozen German motor-torpedo-boats laying mines caused serious shipping losses in the final months of the war. By this time the German air force had greatly reduced its mine-laying activity (being wrongly employed instead in air-launching the very first cruise missiles, the 'flying bombs', against England), but the German E-boats (small, fast torpedo-gunboats) operated from their Dutch bases until the very end of the war. Air bombing was ineffective against them, nor did the vigorous offensive patrols of British light coastal craft eliminate the menace. The main defence comprised convoy escorts, as always; and many additional destroyers, frigates and corvettes, some hastily withdrawn from other naval commands at home and abroad, patrolled the swept channels off the east coast and in the approaches to the River Schelde. A refinement of tactics involved each destroyer or frigate patrolling in company with two motor-torpedo-boats under shore control. The destroyer provided the formidable fire-power which the E-boat forces feared and a higher and steadier radar platform. Some frigates had the latest radar, which could detect an E-boat at 7 miles' range, and in such a vessel a control officer with coastal forces experience would direct the motor-torpedo-boats by radio to intercept the E-boats. Meanwhile, obsolescent aircraft, slow and therefore well suited to the task, flew patrols over the narrow sea, attacking with bombs any radar contacts of E-boats, but more important, reporting to Nore Command at Sheerness; thus a plot could be kept on shore and in every destroyer. Beside the plotters in the destroyer's tiny, dimly lit charthouse, the German-speaking 'headache operator' listened continually to the enemy's radio traffic, hoping to glean intelligence of his plans.

Even against such powerful and well co-ordinated defences, however, the small E-boat force, the coastal submarines and the tiny midget submarines made the last few months of the European war, as their war narrative puts it, 'Nore Command's most anxious time since the Germans' attempt to block the Thames Estuary at the end of 1939'. The narrative continues: 'The Schelde approaches were thick with midget submarines, the E-boats were still showing great persistence and the number of wrecks in the vital channel to the Schelde was steadily increasing.'

So we come to the end of this excursion into the controversial convoy story, in which the fleet destroyer had played a notable part even though she was neither designed nor suitable for such work. Having taken the shock of the first two years of the second Battle of the Atlantic, the fleet destroyer returned to the stage to play a part that was more like the one for which she had been intended; other, more suitable ships were built, manned (largely by amateurs) and trained for the escort task. Indeed, what we have described as perhaps the Royal Navy's greatest campaign of them all had been fought by a predominantly civilian force of reservists, manning twenty-year-old destroyers converted for long-range escort work and anti-submarine warfare, or the tiny corvettes or, later, the frigates. Coastal convoys were likewise left to old destroyers and to the small Hunt-class destroyers, frigates and corvettes, again manned chiefly by reservists and 'hostilities only' officers and ratings. The concept of the battle-fleet, now reduced to the battle-squadron, remained. A small squadron of battleships had been despatched to the Pacific Fleet, and although the fast carrier striking force had inherited the crown of the battle-fleet, the fleet destroyer was still in demand as escort to the aircraft-carrier. Each carrier would be closely attended by fast fleet destroyers, which gave anti-submarine escort and additional anti-aircraft fire-power against low-level air attack.

The fleet destroyer had by now assumed some of the functions of the light cruiser and was constantly in action, fighting her own kind, as at Narvik, as well as cruisers and battleships in the classic manner. The details of their many engagements make stirring reading, and it is easy to see why destroyer men would not have wished to serve in any other class of ship. Destroyers attacked the battleship *Bismarck* with torpedoes, and the battleship *Littorio*. The little *Glowworm*, alone and hopelessly outgunned, actually rammed the heavy cruiser *Hipper*. The destroyers *Ardent* and *Acasta* fought until overwhelmed by the battle-cruisers *Scharnhorst* and *Gneisenau*, and nearly two years later some of the Royal Navy's oldest destroyers closed to 3000 yards and less to launch their torpedoes at those same battle-cruisers.

On the other side of the world, in the Philippines, Captain J. G. Coward, US Navy, led his five destroyers in a classic torpedo attack on Admiral Nishimura's heavy squadron. At half a minute past three in the morning of 25 October 1944 Coward's ships were making thick, black funnel smoke to screen themselves as they drove at the enemy at 30 knots, steering a zig-zag course as they came under fire. Having closed the range to about 4 miles, they turned away to launch a total of forty-seven torpedoes, scoring hits on five of the enemy ships, of which three were sunk, including one of the battleships.

Just four hours later and 100 miles away, in broad daylight, another small force of American destroyers gallantly covered their escort carriers, now under fire from the guns of four Japanese battleships and eight cruisers, so successfully that only one of the carriers was lost. This heroic fight of the destroyers *Hoel, Johnston* and *Roberts* was their last, for they were all sunk. A Japanese officer wrote: 'The enemy destroyers co-ordinated perfectly to cover the inferior speed of the escort carriers. They bravely launched torpedoes to intercept us, and they embarrassed us by putting up a dense smoke screen.' One of the Japanese heavy cruisers present that day, *Haguro*, was herself caught north of Sumatra many months later by the Twenty-Sixth Destroyer Flotilla (Captain M. L. Power, Royal Navy), which was steaming through the darkness. Radar contact was gained at 34 miles, and the attack began, but *Haguro* reversed her course, and at close range the flotilla leader, *Saumarez*, was hit several times, although she and *Verulam* got off their torpedoes. In avoiding these, the cruiser was torpedoed by destroyers *Venus* and *Virgo*, and at last the cruiser *Exeter*, sunk by that same *Haguro* in the Java Sea three years earlier, was avenged. It was a textbook attack, as taught at the torpedo school HMS *Vernon*, and it was to be the very last action of its kind. So ended the Golden Age of the fleet destroyer, a remarkably simple, uncomplicated age. It had lasted half a century and had been illuminated by excitement and courage.

There will always remain the task for which the destroyer had never been designed: the protection of merchant shipping, rather than high-speed work with the fleet. In the years following the Second World War the frigate emerged as a specialist anti-submarine vessel, as an anti-aircraft ship or as an air-defence ship for directing interceptor–fighter aircraft. For some time the business of anti-submarine and anti-aircraft warfare remained much the same, until in the early 1960s came the fast nuclear-powered submarine, the true submarine, and the anti-ship guided or homing missile launched from an aircraft, from a submarine or from another surface vessel. Destroyers and frigates now mounted fewer guns, as anti-aircraft and anti-ship missiles took their place. The only gun that was left had a higher rate of fire, up to seventy rounds a minute, and was fully automatic, firing for three minutes or so without a crew. Anti-missile defence was the job of an anti-missile guided missile and of 20mm or 35mm cannon with rates of fire up to 500 rounds a minute. No longer did the captain fight his enemy from the traditional open bridge of the destroyer or frigate; the processing of infinitely more information, provided by much more sophisticated sensors, required computer solutions and visual display units. These had to be below and were located in the operations room between decks, which would henceforward be the ship's command post, from which the battle would be fought—several battles at once, if need be—against submarines, against missiles and aircraft and against other ships.

31 The frigate is more than a helicopter platform: she is the linchpin of anti-submarine warfare.

The destroyer concept was undergoing its greatest transformation; and as reciprocating engines had given way to steam turbines, these were now superseded by the gas turbine for their main machinery. The most dramatic development of the new technological revolution was to be the equipping of quite small destroyer types with their own air power. In the helicopter the navy had at last found a fast, long-range weapons and sensor platform. The helicopter, which in turn has acquired the ideal platform at sea, complementary to itself, can be directed from the parent frigate to the vicinity of the detected submarine, where it can lower its own sonar to search for and locate the target both for itself and for its parent ship. Attacks can be made with homing torpedoes on its own information or on command, and the 'chopper' can also launch guided missiles against surface craft. The frigate is much more than an expensive helicopter launching and recovery pad; she is also a long-range communications station, a sensor platform, a floating command post from which several different situations can be appreciated on the spot, at sea, rather than from a headquarters thousands of miles away. She is, in short, a multi-purpose, anti-submarine, anti-aircraft, anti-missile, anti-surface-ship weapons system; she can even bombard shore targets or land a company of marines and sailors in an internal security role for good measure.

No war is quite like the one before, even though the second Battle of the Atlantic bore a strong resemblance to the unrestricted submarine warfare of 1917–18. While communications are the all-important prerequisite for success in any conflict, the frigate's tasks in the growing field of electronic warfare are assuming greater importance and explain the boxy superstructure of the modern destroyer or frigate. Electronic equipment, and that for command, control and communications, requires numerous large aerial arrays high above the waterline for greatest efficiency. This design shift reflects the changing nature of any future war at sea. The Second World War torpedo had an effective range of 2 miles or so, and its launching platform, the diesel-electric submersible, had to be in a favourable position for attack, even when launching the first homing torpedoes. The modern torpedo has a range several times greater and is a missile with its own built-in guidance and homing systems, which can be launched on, over or under the sea. Anti-ship missiles can be launched from aircraft with ranges of 200 or 300 miles, and the technology marches forward day by day. The ocean battleground will be much bigger. The 7-knot convoy of thirty, forty or sixty ships, escorted by half a dozen destroyers and corvettes, will mostly be replaced by a few large container ships and tankers steaming at 18 to 20 knots. The convoy concept and the need for close escort will require a very different destroyer type in view of all these major changes. In one other respect the opening stages of a war against the shipping of NATO would be different: today there is afloat a great tonnage of shipping under the flag of Third World nations, whose neutrality might be important to an aggressor. In the face of these changed circumstances, and given the huge numbers of attack submarines available to the Soviet Union, it seems clear that there can be no holds barred in the daunting task of containing them. Great importance must attach to denying them access to the historic battleground of the North Atlantic. An important exit to close is that from the Norwegian Sea, either via the Denmark Strait between Greenland and Iceland or through the Iceland–Faroes gap. These 'choke points', like the one off North Cape, afford an opportunity to detect and monitor the passage of potential enemy submarines and surface ships in peacetime and to destroy them in wartime; it is here that the 'hunting groups' of large frigates carrying two helicopters apiece and aircraft-carriers, including such fleet carriers as remain and the new 'Harrier carriers', would clearly be of great value. The long-range maritime patrol aircraft, now with good detection equipment and weapons to match, and the attack submarine complete the team on which the success of future anti-submarine operations will depend.

The concept of the destroyer is nearly a century old. At first the defender of that very specialized form of convoy, the battle-fleet, and later the 'light cavalry' of the fleet, she has outgrown her offensive weapons and has reverted to a largely defensive role. A hundred years ago the torpedo-boat was the first launching platform for the new defensive weapon, the torpedo. Then came the submarine, then the fast motor-torpedo-boat and the torpedo-boat destroyer herself (the torpedo having become an *offensive* weapon), then the aircraft with torpedo or bomb, and today the guided missile-boat (a cheap launching platform for an expensive weapon of great range, accuracy and destructive power) and, finally, the huge, deep-diving nuclear-powered submarine. The destroyer type which emerged in the early 1890s has survived, perhaps because she is, or should be, of a certain critical size necessary for successful operations on the surface, where the worst weather can be found but where relative slowness is an advantage, and because she provides a stable platform for helicopter-borne missiles and torpedoes and for elaborate sensors and other electronic devices. She is also a floating command post for the co-ordination and control of many types of naval activity, most of which may well fall far short of war. The destroyer type, the smallest practicable 'major war vessel', is therefore likely to last as long as the submarine and the aircraft. Certainly, the destroyer concept has been the most consistent, in sea-power terms, throughout the modern period of tremendous change.

Chapter Nine

THE MAKING OF A NAVY

Navies remain an instrument of statecraft. They also consume enormous amounts of money, employ several million people throughout the world, control terrible destructive potential, and operate in that watery two thirds of the earth's surface which is increasingly a major international issue area.

KEN BOOTH, *Navies and Foreign Policy*, 1979

It is customary to divide the old navy into the battle-fleet, the cruiser squadrons and the 'flotilla vessels'—noting, however, that in the Second World War task forces were formed which included all three main types. Thirty years later, in a nuclear, electronic age, the old idea of a battle-fleet has gone, and the battleship herself has vanished. What is surprising is the longevity of the battle-fleet concept and the battleship in the age of the submarine and the aircraft, and the even longer lifespan of the aircraft-carrier, which actually took the battleship's place in a version of the line of battle (albeit for a few short years) and fought at ranges of hundreds of miles rather than hundreds of yards, as was expected of battleships a century ago. The cruiser's survival in the face of the aircraft which might have been expected to replace her is as astonishing as her resilience in the face of attack from the air. Perhaps the very size of the cruiser inventory in the world's principal navies made it necessary to employ these ships to the limits of prudence and beyond. In retrospect, it seems strange that as recently as the 1940s cruisers should have fought each other at point-blank range in the Pacific, or that Commodore Harwood, far away in the South Atlantic, should have acted like some latter-day Hornblower, utterly dependent on his own intuitive skill and the courage and efficiency of his sailors, or that the only practicable means of reconnaissance in the Denmark Strait should have been a 10,000-ton, heavily armed vessel with a complement of 800. All that is ended, yet the cruiser, now a vastly more powerful weapons platform, remains to patrol the oceans.

If success is to be measured only in terms of destruction achieved, the submarine has been the most successful type of war vessel yet developed. Today the true submarine, the strategic ballistic missile version, is the ultimate form of force projection against an enemy homeland; the older submersible has dominated naval warfare for seventy years, and as yet no complete counter to such underwater craft exists. Given the extent and depth of the oceans and the physical laws governing the transmission of sound through seawater, it seems a reasonable assumption that the submarine will maintain her dominant position for many years to come, but to be truly effective, the submarine requires the protection and co-operation of friendly naval forces both on the surface and in the air. In time of war the submarine cannot safely show herself on the surface, while in peacetime she is quite unsuited to the diversity of tasks that an ocean-going navy must perform in order both to exercise sea power and to confront it.

In the ninety-odd years of the destroyer concept, size has been as important as it was for the battleship. The destroyer superseded the torpedo-boat because, being larger, she could steam faster in bad weather and could out-gun her prey. In later years this critical size was important if she were also to provide a platform for a helicopter hangar and arrays of sensors and enough room for the complex command, control and communications equipment upon which successful naval operations at sea must always depend. In these respects, the problems facing the naval architect are not very different from those with which his grandfather had to deal. A dreadnought's rangefinder, spotting-top and wireless aerials, with her armoured turrets and conning tower, made dangerous top-weight, which could only be corrected by a longer hull, deeper draught and broader beam. While heavy armour has been replaced by better damage control and invisible electronic 'armour', some warship-design problems remain intractable. The enormous weight of shells, far below the waterline, formerly compensated for top-weight, but missile-launchers, though relatively light and with fewer reloads, are on or near the upper deck. The centre of gravity is further raised by the mass of electronic aerials placed as high as possible, rather like a full rig of sail in the early years of steam.

The destroyer, or frigate, is certainly vulnerable to the aircraft and the submarine, but she can dominate the ocean surface where neither submarine nor aircraft can loiter for long in safety. It is at this meeting-point of the elements that all maritime commerce is to be found and a variety of dire events may occur, from inter-continental nuclear war, through conventional war, to the emergencies of constabulary duty—in short, all the occasions for the exercise of sea power. The submarine captain brings his boat to the surface at his peril. The airman must soon return to his base many hundreds of miles away. The ship-borne airman depends utterly on his mobile, floating airfield much nearer. Some critics of the destroyer or frigate favour the small, relatively cheap, missile-launching, fast patrol boat, but such craft are of much less value to a 'blue-water' navy whose battleground is in the North Atlantic or the Norwegian Sea and whose strategy is a defensive one. Merchantmen on the high seas cannot be protected by small missile craft whose electronic sensors and weapons, quite simply, are housed in too small a hull to do the job.

The problem is economic rather than military or technical, and sea power has always rested on a nation's industrial base, as well as on the requirements of its foreign policy. A hundred years ago the Royal Navy, then the world's largest and most powerful, was the creation of the world's greatest and most advanced industrial complex. A skilled workforce and modern foundries, factories and shipyards with up-to-date machines and tools gave Britain a head-start in the naval armaments race that was only just beginning. Steel warships, marine engines, armour-plate, ordnance and control and communications systems could all be provided in plenty, at low cost and quickly. But Britain's technological and industrial lead was to be shorter-lived than anyone then supposed, for we know now that by the end of the nineteenth century (before the direct military challenge from Germany became apparent) British industry and technology were in decline in relation to those of Germany and the United States, while all too soon the newest emergent power, Japan, would also show signs of rivalling the pioneer industrial state. The slow process of decline was concealed by new investment occasioned by two world wars. British yards continued to build ships for Dominion navies, which were thus in varying degrees, integrated with the Royal Navy. British yards also built warships for foreign navies, and they still do, but Britain's industrial base began to shrink, in absolute terms, from around 1970. (It may be noted that a similar lack of capacity and the specialist skills of drawing office and workbench slowed naval rearmament in the 1930s.)

Even after the First World War the decline in Britain's industrial health and its swift impact on military performance had been masked by the sheer size of the fleet and by some limited trade protection. The chemicals industry for high explosives, the optical industry for rangefinders, the watch-making industry for shell fuses were all to be protected by tariffs, since the navy that had for so long defended free trade had become, by awful paradox, its victim. The lack of a broad, powerful industrial base, continually modernized and backed by science, weakened British defence directly. A generally poor performance by important sectors of the economy results in a small gross domestic product and a correspondingly smaller tax revenue for defence. No amount of professional skill and courage—amply displayed by the Royal Navy in the twentieth century—can compensate for economic and technical weakness, which promptly shows itself in fewer warships and weapons. Membership of an alliance may help to mitigate or conceal the extent of the deficiency, but a nation that cannot (or will not) pay its way in defence will soon be relegated to the status of junior partner. This is the harsh reality faced by the nation that was once the world's greatest naval power.

For a maritime nation a navy is not a luxury but a necessity. A country dependent in large measure on the free movement of the world's merchant marine needs the assurance that its shipping and ports can be defended. The debate is no less intense, and a good deal more urgent, than it was a hundred years ago. The recurring 'navy scare' of the 1880s and 1890s, the arguments about size and number of battleships (or whether to have them at all), the merits of the torpedo-boat, the fears of French or Russian or German construction programmes—all have a familiar ring today. In Britain even the politics of naval Estimates have an up-to-date flavour if one recalls the (quite unfounded) suggestion at the turn of the century that Liberal Governments were less generous to the Royal Navy than their Conservative opponents! Today the debate is about the cost-effectiveness of the aircraft-carrier, the submarine and the destroyer or frigate. It is also about our most appropriate, as well as our most useful, contribution to a great alliance pledged to defence by deterrence, for we can no longer meet the challenge alone. Of one thing we can be certain: our potential enemies at least understand the importance of sea power, and we shall forget it at our peril.

Chapter Ten

EPILOGUE

House of Lords, 20 July 1981. The Lord President of the Council moved 'That this House takes note of the White Paper "The United Kingdom Defence Programme—the Way Forward" '. At 3.46 p.m. The Lord Hill-Norton rose and said:

'My Lords, we are asked by the noble Lord the Lord President to take note of the White Paper. It would be difficult, for me at least, not to do so, since it represents the second attempt by a Tory Government to destroy the Royal Navy, in the last twenty-four years. It will not, therefore, surprise your Lordships if I address most of my remarks today to what is now so foolishly proposed for the service whose uniform I have worn for more than fifty years.

'But, before doing so, it would only be fair to welcome certain aspects of the White Paper. I concede with pleasure that an attempt has been made, for the first time for many years, to carry out a Defence Review on the right basis, even if it has been constrained from the beginning by a fixed monetary ceiling, arbitrarily chosen, and quite unrelated to geo-political, much less military, requirements. The fact that the Government have arrived at the wrong solution is their fault, and not the fault of the method. I shall say where and why I think they have got the wrong answers.

'I feel constrained to remark first on the management of defence, for the changes so recently made in ministerial responsibilities seem to me a wholly retrograde step, by detaching the Parliamentary Under-Secretaries of State from the three individual services, apparently, or so the announcement implied, for fear that they might become too closely identified with their single service as opposed to defence as a whole. Surely the whole object of appointing the service

Ministers always has been to represent the point of view of services of which they acquire detailed knowledge, and of the men and women in them, both to Parliament and to the Cabinet.

'We have two greatly distinguished former First Lords of the Admiralty in your Lordships' House and, having served under both of them, I can recall no instance in which their loyalties were divided to the point of embarrassment to the Government of the day; indeed, I have always supposed that the reverse was true. Loyalty can exist only when members of any team share a belief in their objectives, and share a determination to achieve them; it can certainly not be ordained, much less organized. I find it a regrettable sign of weakness by the Government that such an attempt should have been made. Management, and more important to the armed forces of the Crown, leadership, will be the poorer for it.

'I turn from the general to the particular. The Government's thinking—if I may so dignify the process—seems to be based on several demonstrably false assumptions, which flow almost certainly from sheer ignorance of the total defence problem. There is no doubt some political adroitness in what is before us, but no intellectual consistency, much less any sign that strategic realities have been studied and measures appropriate to deter them or to deal with them have been devised. I am not alone in this view of the White Paper as a whole, for it was described in the other place two weeks ago as:

> "faulty in reasoning, incomplete in strategy and totally mysterious in arithmetic"—

and so it is, as I shall seek to show. That is not really surprising, partly in the light of what I have just said about management; partly by the very short acquaintance with the subject of the Ministers now responsible; and partly from a dogged refusal to accept the advice of those who are constitutionally responsible for giving it. I refer, of course, to the Chiefs of Staff who have felt obliged to exercise their right to represent their anxiety about this review to the Prime Minister twice in the last six months. I do not believe that that has happened before in this century.

'The three most damaging false assumptions to which I have referred are, first, that any future war in Europe will be short and therefore the problem of reinforcement and re-supply across the Atlantic is of secondary importance; which wholly misunderstands the concept of deterrence. Secondly, that if we abandon the NATO task in the North Atlantic someone else will do our job for us; which no other European ally can, and the Americans are already so overstretched that they will not do so. Thirdly, that the job of surface warships in the Atlantic can be done by maritime aircraft and submarines; indeed, the White Paper at paragraph 26 actually says:

> "Our most powerful vessels for maritime war are our nuclear-propelled attack submarines."

'I do not agree with that view, and I know of no other war-experienced practising sailor who does do so. I have heard of some superficial, so-called scientific, theories upon which the Government's view may well be based, despite the complete lack of any operational or even experimental evidence in support of them. I may be forgiven for preferring a widely-shared professional opinion of how best to deter, or if that fails, to fight a war at sea.

'I should like to deal briefly with the first two of those false assumptions. Before remarking in more detail upon the effect of the White Paper proposals upon the Royal Navy, I must say at once that deterrence to all war, nuclear or conventional, long or short, is indivisible. It is as much in the mind of an aggressor, as it is in our own. It applies as much in the Atlantic as it does in the central region of NATO, or as it does outside the NATO area. It depends critically upon a flexible response, enshrined from the outset in the North Atlantic Treaty. There is no scenario to which an Allied response, and hence our own defence policy, could be seen to be adequate, which can be based upon a short war. The United States Secretary of Defense, Mr Weinberger, said only a few weeks ago:

> "The idea that all future wars will be short has been overtaken by events."

Nor is the short war notion any part of NATO doctrine; and it is hard to see how anyone in the West planning for such a war, is planning to do anything but lose it. I need hardly remind your Lordships that both the last World Wars were expected by politicians, and thus by the public—on both sides—to be short wars. Nor need I remind your Lordships that we came very close to defeat in both of them; in the battles of the Atlantic.

'As for the notion that somebody else will pick up the tab in the North Atlantic; we now provide 70 per cent of all the Allied forces there deployed, for 20 per cent of our defence budget, and we provide 10 per cent of the land air forces in the Central Region for 40 per cent of our defence budget. There simply is no other ally with the means to do the maritime job. Moreover, our allies expect us to do it, and the Supreme Allied Commander Atlantic has recently stated that his escort ship strength is even now only 50 per cent of what he considers the necessary minimum. The United States Department of Defence report for fiscal year 1982 states:

> "the powerful and operationally effective Royal Navy provides the bulk of the non-U.S. contribution".

The International Herald Tribune recently commented:

> "if British ships are taken out of service, there are no other allied naval forces to replace them. The US Navy is stretched so thin, and is so undermanned at the moment, that it could not possibly fill the gap."

The same paper goes on to say:

> "cuts in British naval strength will weaken the alliance's capability to fight a prolonged conventional war in Europe".

'One might have supposed that the Government were unaware of these simple truths; but when agreeing with a statement in another place recently that

> "the principal role of the Royal Navy is to keep open the North Atlantic for reinforcement and re-supply, without which we could not survive",

the Defence Secretary declared only two months ago:

> "I entirely agree that a vital factor in any war on the central front will be the reinforcement of NATO, much of which will need to be done by sea"

—he might have said, more accurately, 95 per cent of which will have to be done by sea. NATO, as Melvin Laird said when he was the United States Defence Secretary, is "an Alliance strung together by ships". Reductions in our surface fleet must, in all these circumstances, strike at the very cohesion of the alliance upon which our whole defence policy is based.

'What then is left of these ill-advised proposals, and what will be the outcome if they are given effect? It can only be the absurd notion, to which I have already referred, that the Atlantic life line can be kept open by maritime aircraft and submarines. I imagine that some of your Lordships may have seen Captain Stephen Roskill's comments on this foolish assessment, in his letter to *The Times* last month. No one in the country is a greater authority on naval warfare, and he described what is now proposed as the height of folly.

'The mysterious arithmetic, to which I have already referred, was much discussed in the debate two weeks ago in another place. It appears, though it is far from clear, that the intention is to reduce our destroyer and frigate force from fifty-nine ships, three of which are in reserve, to fifty ships, of which eight will be in reserve, or from fifty-six to forty-two. This is a huge reduction, but the facts may well be much worse. Mr Speed, who has very good reason to know them, has asserted that twenty-six ships will be disposed of in the next three or four years, with perhaps nine coming forward in the same time-scale. Whatever the truth may be—and I can understand the Government's reluctance to reveal it in plain terms—it seems clear enough that the operational escort fleet will be reduced by between 25 and 35 per cent.

'The White Paper suggests that ample compensation will be made by adding three Nimrod aircraft, five nuclear-powered submarines (which represent no addition, because they were in the programme already) and some newly-designed diesel submarines arriving at the rate of one a year, starting about six years from now. I find it inconceivable that anyone, much less the responsible Ministers, could believe that such a preposterous rate of exchange could leave our capability unimpaired. It certainly cannot fail to reduce our capability to deter the Soviet fleet outside the NATO area, to which the White Paper rightly accords some priority. Moreover, it takes no account at all of the loss of some twenty helicopters, which fly from the destroyers and frigates, each of which is nearly as good an anti-submarine weapons system.

'Maritime warfare today is a team business; surface ships, submarines, ship-borne aircraft, and maritime aircraft, each have a part to play. Grossly to reduce any one element of that team fatally unbalances the whole, and an arbitrary decision on our part to change the shape of this allied deterrent in the North Atlantic makes nonsense of our emphasis on defence through the NATO Alliance.

'I might perhaps add here that of the twenty new ships

coming into service in the next five years, to which the White Paper gives some prominence, less than half are destroyers and frigates—the rest being mine counter-measures vessels and submarines—and that of the twenty ships concerned, fifteen were ordered by the last Labour Government and only five by this Administration, of which just one is a major war vessel. To compound the folly, the Government propose to complete the last two big ships of the "*Invincible*" class, and then dispose of one of the three, thus paying their high capital costs and failing to reap the reward of their very low running costs, when they are ideally suited, and unmatched by any other Navy in the Alliance, for both Atlantic and out-of-area operations.

'I must, before concluding, say a few words about Trident. As your Lordships are aware, I am totally convinced that the Government are right to go forward with this corner-stone of our defence policy, and there is no need for me to rehearse my reasons again. They were put cogently and briefly by Marshal of the Royal Air Force Sir William Dickson in a letter to *The Times* a few weeks ago, and it is more than a coincidence that his views are shared by three other former Chiefs of the Defence Staff; leaving the noble and gallant Lord, Lord Carver, in a dissenting minority of one against four.

'The proposition which the noble and gallant Lord has put to your Lordships in the past—and for all I know he may well do so again today—that an armament of immense power, unique in its politico-military nature, is of less strategic value than a necessarily modest increase in conventional forces, is certainly not self-evidently true, even if the noble Lord, Lord Gladwyn, and perhaps some other noble Lords, also believe it. In my view the very reverse is true; and the critics of the programme have lost the argument. What is depressing about it, to me, is that the repeated assurances that Ministers have given to Parliament that the Trident programme would not diminish our conventional forces, now seem to have been abandoned so far as the Navy is concerned. I find it even more depressing that last year we looked our American friends in the eye and told them that we would not be cutting our surface fleet to pay for Trident. Indeed, I have understood from the published papers, that we obtained very generous terms from them, on the basis of that assurance, which has now plainly been broken. I am glad that it was not my word which was given.

'I have spoken at greater length than usual, and greater length than the noble Lord the Lord President invited us to, because, for me, this is an unusual occasion. There are, however, two further points about the Royal Navy which I must mention briefly. The White Paper says that more naval training will be done at sea, rather than ashore. It is probably news for the Government that this has been tried before, only about ten years ago; and it was shown not to work and to cost much more. Nor is any account taken in the White Paper of career structures; the vital importance of officers and sailors obtaining sea-going experience; and the whole morale of a service which is to lose 15 per cent of its trained manpower. What, if any, thought have the Government given to problems of this nature? No doubt they will leave their solution to the professionals, whose advice on operational matters they have so arrogantly rejected. Thank goodness that we have immensely competent senior officers to make the best of this very bad job.

'To conclude, I regard these savage cuts in the Royal Navy as a highly dangerous gamble with our national security. They flow from a misunderstanding of the threat, ignorance of the best means to counter it, disregard for the combined capability of the Alliance, a mistaken assessment of priorities and a total neglect of history. War may be, as Talleyrand said, too serious a business for the generals; but defence policy certainly seems too difficult a business for this Government. I am appalled by what is proposed; I am affronted by the way it has been done; and I am deeply concerned about the almost certain consequences.'

After fifty-three years in the Royal Navy I could have said much more—but could hardly have said less.

INDEX